108th U.S. Open Championship

Torrey Pines Golf Course

June 12-16, 2008

108th
U.S. OPEN
Torrey Pines
Golf Course

Written by David Shedloski   Photography by Getty Images   Edited by Bev Norwood

ISBN 1-878843-54-0

©2008 United States Golf Association®
Golf House, Far Hills, N.J. 07931

Statistics produced by IBM

Photographs ©Getty Images
Photographs on pages 1, 7, 8, 13 and 17 ©USGA/John Mummert
Course illustrations by Dan Wardlaw ©The Majors of Golf

Published by IMG Worldwide Inc.,
1360 East Ninth Street, Cleveland, Ohio 44114

Designed and produced by Davis Design

Printed in the United States of America

Some U.S. Open Championships become forgettable in time. Not the 2008 edition. Not a chance. Drama reigned throughout the week as the United States Golf Association displayed once again that its revered championship, held for so many years on private country club courses, can be, should be and will be staged on some of our nation's excellent public facilities from time to time. Golf is a game of all the people.

The path to Tiger Woods' third Open triumph and 14th major victory, remarkable in itself, became much more so when it was learned that the injuries he nursed that week at San Diego's toughened-up municipal Torrey Pines Golf Course were so serious that within days after the win he underwent surgery that ended his 2008 season.

Tiger never ceases to impress me with his talent, his wonderful physical condition and his mental strength. Here was a man who played in pain through 91 grueling holes in the most important golf championship in the world, who made the critical shots and clutch putts he had to make to stay alive long enough to put the finishing touches on the victory in California.

The drama was not provided by Woods alone. Rocco Mediate, a good friend whom I have known since he was a teenager in our home area in Western Pennsylvania, challenged Tiger to the wire, never flinching until the very end. Rocco, who has had an injury-plagued, up-and-down career, maintained his free-spirited demeanor throughout the final round of the championship and the playoff, hanging tough even when things seemed to be slipping away from him on the second nine Sunday.

They say that nobody remembers who finished second in a golf tournament. I don't think that will be the case with the 2008 U.S. Open and Rocco Mediate. Granted that Tiger was on the shelf with the injury and impending surgery, but name another runner-up in any sport who received the sort of national media attention than Rocco did in the days after Torrey Pines.

This publication, the 24th in the series presented by Rolex, truly deserves its place in the library of any follower of the great game of golf.

Arnold Palmer

A view of the South Course at Torrey Pines featuring the second, third and fifth greens and third and fourth tees.

108th
U.S. OPEN
Torrey Pines
Golf Course

The South Course at Torrey Pines didn't seem, at first glance, like a worthy choice for the United States Golf Association to hold its premier event. At first glance. But the well-trafficked municipal golf course without a substantial pedigree or much critical acclaim welcomed the 108th U.S. Open Championship radiating a munificence that belied its muscular profile.

Sprawled atop scenic coastal bluffs offering stunning views of the Pacific Ocean, Torrey South, as people in and around San Diego call it, made up for whatever it lacked in aura with a straightforward examination of bedrock USGA parameters amid one of the most invigorating upland golfing properties in the world. Torrey Pines became only the second municipal—and first city-owned—golf course to host the national Open, and it was the first to garner such an honor without a seal of approval from one or another list of the top 100 courses in the United States.

Architect William P. Bell, whose design credits include local golf courses Balboa Park, La Jolla Country Club and San Diego Country Club, designed both the North and South Courses at Torrey Pines, but he died in 1953 before much work was completed. His son, William F. Bell, went to work on the courses in 1957, and Torrey Pines opened a year later with a celebrated group first off the tees. In that inaugural round were former U.S. Open champions Ralph Guldahl and Olin Dutra and two-time PGA Tour winner Paul Runyan, who was La Jolla Country Club's head professional at the time. In fact, Torrey South's hosting of its first major championship occurred one week before the 50th anniversary of its debut.

Just six years earlier, in 2002, Bethpage State Park's Black Course in Farmingdale, N.Y., had become the first municipal facility to be deemed worthy to host the national Open, but Bethpage (which hosts the Open again in 2009) was considered a largely overlooked A.W. Tillinghast-designed gem that was long overdue to be included among the venues staging America's grandest golf event.

Torrey Pines, named after the distinctive conifer that grows along the cliffs, was among the golfing aficionados best known for being the home since 1969 of a PGA Tour event, presently the Buick Invitational, and the annual site of the Junior World Golf Championship that spawned numerous promising players, including current world-ranked No. 1 Tiger Woods, the 2000 and 2002 U.S. Open champion; world No. 2 Phil Mickelson and world No. 4 Ernie Els, the South African who won the 1994 and 1997 U.S. Opens. Torrey Pines also hosted the 1998 U.S. Amateur Public Links Championship, which was won by another South African talent, Trevor Immelman, who would come to the 2008 U.S. Open after holding off Woods to win the Masters Tournament.

Perched some 300 feet above the shoreline, Torrey Pines also was known outside golf circles as a popular site for parasailing and for nearby Black's Beach, a clothing-optional destination for the less inhibited sun worshipers in Southern California.

Bethpage Black had changed the perception of what constituted a proper Open golf course. It took the energy and foresight of Jay Rains and Rich Gillette to change the perception of Torrey South. Members of the Century Club, the not-for-profit

1st
PAR 4
448 YARDS

charitable organization that manages the Buick Invitational, Rains (who now serves on the USGA's Executive Committee) and Gillette spearheaded a fund-raising initiative aimed at bringing the South Course up to major championship standards, and they brought in Rees Jones to oversee what would become a $3.3 million renovation.

The choice of Jones couldn't have been more appropriate considering that Jones is known as the "Open Doctor," a moniker he inherited from his legendary architect father, Robert Trent Jones. His thoughtful approach to upgrading classic designs in today's technologically fueled era has made Jones a popular choice for renovating or retouching classics like Bethpage Black, Baltusrol's Lower Course, Congressional Country Club's Blue Course, Hazeltine National Golf Club, East Lake Golf Club and Medinah's No. 3 Course. In all, Jones has renovated seven Open layouts, and another of his 70 renovation efforts was going to be on display in August at the PGA Championship at Oakland Hills Country Club, near Detroit.

When Jones was finished with Torrey South, Bell's routing, benign but mundane as it ran astride the accompanying canyons, was left intact, but the par-72 golf course (converted to par 71 for the Open) had been beefed up to 7,643 yards. That made it not only the longest Open lay-

out in history—by 379 yards—but also the longest in major championship golf, surpassing Augusta National Golf Club at 7,445 yards and relegating the 7,536-yard Straits Course at Whistling Straits in Wisconsin, site of the 2004 PGA Championship, to second place.

But Jones did much more than turn a standard automobile into a stretch limousine. He built new tees and rebuilt the greens complexes to enlarge them and give them more character and strategic value with plateaus, terraces and ridges. A couple of the complexes he moved closer to canyons or the edges of the cliffs, such as at the downhill par-3 third hole and the scenic par-4 fourth, where he also shifted the fairway left, closer to the bluff. The only other green pushed nearer a falloff was at the par-4 14th hole. Finally, Jones added more than 60 bunkers, repositioned some bunkers to tighten landing areas, and he also had the bunkers deepened to be more penal, especially around the greens.

Predictably, the field scoring average at the Buick Invitational increased by more than two strokes during its encounter after being put back together with Rees's pieces.

"The strategy of playing Torrey Pines' South Course has been dramatically changed," said Jones, age 66, who did the major renovation work in 2001 but admitted that he

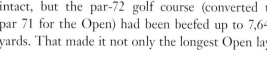

2nd
PAR 4
389 YARDS

The third hole, par 3 and 142 to 195 yards.

had been tweaking it a bit each year leading up to the Open. "We repositioned greens to bring in the natural hazards of the ocean cliffs and the canyons. Most greens have alternate approaches of attack to an open entrance or to a fortified hole location. We redesigned the greens with challenging transitions that allow for small targets within the larger surface.

"Green contours, terraces and small 'tongues' that drift on a diagonal serve to protect hole locations. This puts a risk/reward option in the hands of the U.S. Open contestants. Being near the hole is almost essential for making birdies, while playing to the fat of the green will almost surely end up

3rd
PAR 3
142/195 YARDS

in a two-putt and a par. We also rebuilt the bunkers, repositioning them and making them deeper. Their shapes and slopes will render an unpredictable lie from a player's errant shot."

Jones was intent on better utilizing the immense space on the South Course without tearing it up and starting over. He also wanted to better utilize the space on the greens to confound today's players. It wasn't the first time the greens had been redone. They died early in the course's life when sand from the beach was used to fill the bunkers and the accompanying sea salt initiated their demise. In the early 1970s, San Diegan Billy Casper, a former Masters

7

The fourth hole, par 4 and 448 to 488 yards.

and two-time U.S. Open champion, was brought in to re-engineer them to help them drain better. Among his improvements was removing leftover asphalt upon which some of them had been built.

Jones' plans for changing the greens also were out of

4th
PAR 4
448/488 YARDS

necessity, but his intention was to cause a greater degree of brain drain.

"In decades past, the best players ran the ball to the hole," Jones said. "They would hit an approach shot to the green, then let the ball roll toward the hole. Modern players spin the ball a lot more. They don't hit shots that release to the hole; they hit it right at the hole."

Jones wanted them to think twice before firing at the flagsticks. "Shot options … that is why Torrey Pines is a great course for the everyday player and a true test and challenge for the world's best golfers," he said. "It's all about thinking and analyzing your shot."

That Torrey Pines had a shot at garnering an Open and ended up snagging the prize was further surprising in light of the fact that Riviera Coun-

5th
PAR 4
453 YARDS

6th
PAR 4
515 YARDS

7th
PAR 4
461 YARDS

was among those applauding the USGA the loudest. That would be Mickelson.

"As a kid we dreamed and hoped that a major championship would come to Southern California, and the ideal spot would be Torrey Pines," said Mickelson, who four times had been a runner-up in the Open heading into the 2008 championship. "With the redesign six or seven years ago, that dream became a reality. I can't believe this is the U.S. Open Championship here at Torrey Pines. It's something we've dreamed about."

The renovation of Torrey South was only half the story of the verdant examination that was expected to battle and befuddle the best play-

try Club, near Los Angeles, also was a serious contender. Riviera, site of the PGA Tour's Northern Trust Open, formerly known as the Los Angeles Open, is a revered layout from the Golden Age of golf course architecture. It twice hosted the PGA Championship, in 1983 and 1995, as well as the 1948 U.S. Open, and it is famously referred to as "Hogan's Alley," in honor of Ben Hogan, who in a two-year period won the first of his record-tying four U.S. Open titles as well as two Los Angeles Open crowns.

The U.S. Open had not been to Southern California since then, and some eyebrows were raised when Torrey Pines emerged with the bid. Not everyone was surprised, however. A local man who played recreational golf as well as high school matches on both the South and North Courses at Torrey Pines

ers in the world. Another portion of the equation was left in the capable hands of Mike Davis, senior director of rules and competitions for the USGA, in conjunction with Vice President Jim Hyler and the USGA championship committee. The challenge for Davis was to devise a setup that reflected the philosophy of the USGA and in so doing brought about a change in the strategic worth of a layout that was a decent challenge but hardly menaced PGA Tour players who invaded each winter.

Torrey South was the third course on the current professional schedule to host a Tour event and a major championship in the same year, joining Riviera and Pebble Beach Golf Links, and many Open competitors had plenty of time to familiarize themselves with the reconstituted Jones creation

9

The sixth hole, par 4 and 515 yards.

that was relatively soft and bereft of rough during the late January or early February dates for the Buick Invitational.

The warmer, drier weather of mid-June abetted Davis and the championship committee in presenting a wholly different kind of test for the Open, though one still adhering to the overall USGA philosophy that had been established formally in the 1950s and hadn't been altered much since Richard Tufts, then president of the USGA, formulated a blueprint. That plan called for the fastest conditions possible with narrow fairways, penal rough and fast-putting greens—the essential elements to test all aspects of a player's shotmaking abilities and course management skills under extreme physical and psychological duress.

No surprise, then, that Davis wanted to have firmer fairways. He wanted rough that would, depending on the quality of the shot, stymie strategy, alter it or simply offer no solace whatsoever to those who wandered too far afield. And he wanted the saucer-top greens at Torrey Pines running at

speeds up to 13 on the Stimpmeter and decidedly firm though not of concrete consistency.

Two days before the championship, Jones, a soft-spoken man with a keen eye for detail, who had studied history at Yale and design at Harvard, couldn't help but focus his attention on the speed and firmness of his rebuilt greens, which had a few years before the championship been switched from bentgrass to Poa *annua* under the direction of course superintendent Mark Woodward. The putting surfaces had been watered on the Sunday before championship week, and with the misty "June Gloom," a marine layer of light fog that keeps moisture in the air—and on the course—hovering over Torrey Pines, Jones was concerned that the greens might be too soft and receptive and not a proper examination for Open shotmaking.

Jones had seen a similar mistake in the not-too-distant past when Medinah No. 3 was nourished too enthusiastically for the 2006 PGA Championship, and Woods and others played darts for four days. Woods led a bludgeoning of the proud course

8th
PAR 3
177 YARDS

9th
PAR 5
612 YARDS

10th
PAR 4
414 YARDS

rent and past players, Davis undertook a few subtle departures from his initial instincts on the setup of a course that was given a 79.7 course rating and 153 slope rating by the Southern California Golf Association, making it, by simple numerical comparison, one of the hardest in the country. (So it did end up cracking one top-100 list after all.)

Most significantly, the fairway widths remained at around 29-33 yards, similar to what players encounter during the Buick Invitational and decidedly more generous than the 24 yards or so that had been routine at other Open courses. In fact, four fairways had even been widened a bit. That development led several players to remark that they had never seen a more congenial look to an Open course from the tee. There appeared to be plenty of room, and

originally designed by Tom Bendelow, winning his third PGA title by five strokes at 18 under par. Another 39 players rode his coattails and finished under par.

"With the fairways a little more generous than at previous Opens, it's imperative that greens are firm and rolling," said Jones, who has more than 100 original designs to his credit. "That has been the intent all along. Otherwise, you need to have the fairways more narrow and the rough a little higher. You don't want to see the players hitting shots out of the rough and holding. That doesn't help identify the best players, and it's not what we tried to do here when we redesigned it. The philosophy from the start was to work from the starting point of what's needed to have an Open."

After receiving input from cur-

even more given the renewing of the use of graduated rough heights.

A mixture of ryegrass, Poa *annua* and kikuyugrass, the rough was cut in bands of three heights: a first cut of 1-3/4 inches for a width of two yards on either side; a first cut of primary rough that recently was allowed to grow 1/4 inch higher to 2-1/2 inches; and a primary rough of 3 inches and higher to penalize the most inaccurate drives. Davis, a fine golfer in his own right, introduced the graduated rough concept in 2006 at Winged Foot, and believes it has introduced an additional element of fairness to the examination. A player who missed the short kikuyugrass fairways by a little should get a better chance than the wild driver to advance the ball toward the green.

"The theory of graduated rough is that the first cut of primary rough takes away some spin and distance control, but not as much as for those who are wild off the tee," Davis said. "In theory, we like the concept. We wanted to give these players who just miss the fairway the opportunity to demonstrate their skill as shotmakers, and we think they will still be able to do that."

It all depended on the lie, which tended to be unpredictable.

11th
PAR 3
204/221 YARDS

nia, we know all about it. It is a very difficult grass that, to get your club through, takes a very aggressive swing. And there's a certain technique to it. It takes a certain amount of practice, especially around the greens, to have a better idea of how that ball might come out of the kikuyu."

Added Mickelson: "Although it looks like the most playable rough that we've ever had in an Open, it still … what's the word? It's hard to gauge, I guess. Some [shots] come out hot, some come out dead. You just don't know how, out of that first primary cut, the ball is going to come out. And so it's very difficult to be confident going at a green or at a pin."

While five over par had been the winning scores at the two previous U.S. Opens at Winged Foot Golf Club and Oakmont Country Club, Davis didn't arrive at Torrey Pines seeking a similar scoring range. Rough was just one of the barriers to higher scoring at both those venues.

Davis can't say he's a fan of it, per se. He, too, would prefer to see

12th
PAR 4
475/504 YARDS

No matter what height, the choice of kikuyugrass for fairways and rough was important for the Open. Kikuyu is a very tough strand of grass, and it is dominant in Southern California. Trimmed to fairway height, its aggressive runners help the ball rest on top of its blades. It allows for the most gorgeous lies. In the rough, however, it can be exceedingly ugly and punitive; it can be more wiry than bluegrass, rye or even bermudagrass, grabbing and twisting clubs that try to cut through it. Kikuyu is "bermuda on steroids," said USGA president Jim Vernon, who hails from Pasadena, Calif.

"It's a fairly broad leaf and a very tough leaf. It is a very thick, wiry grass," Vernon added. "For those of us who play golf here in Southern Califor-

13th
PAR 5
614 YARDS

The 13th hole, par 5 and 614 yards.

skill come to the fore on more than just swipes from the short grass.

"After Oakmont," Davis said, "I sent a memo to superintendents saying, 'If you think the USGA is looking for incredibly consistent, dense rough, you're mistaken.' We like the idea of a bit of inconsistency in the rough, to give the guys different kinds of shots."

To that same end, the collars of rough around the greens were mowed in concentric steps, and the approach areas in front of greens, which were bermudagrass rather than the kikuyu elsewhere on the fairways, were aerified and top-dressed like the putting surfaces to make them more firm and to promote the idea that approach shots needn't always fly onto the greens. This gave players another option to consider when pondering how to reach the large Poa *annua* greens that Davis wanted to have running two feet faster than they do during the Tour stop.

The final part of the equation was the selection of the teeing grounds, an element of the setup equation that showed the flexibility that Davis has brought to the process and the versatility of the South Course after Jones' revisions. Hyler, the chairman of the championship committee, assured that the course would not play to its full length on any one day, and he kept his

14th
PAR 4
267/435 YARDS

15th
PAR 4
478 YARDS

word. During the fourth round the course was a mere 7,280 yards.

Three separate teeing grounds were used on the par-5 13th hole, which measured anywhere from 530 yards to 614 yards. The USGA also had plans for the par-4 14th hole, normally 435 yards. On Sunday, and again on Monday in the playoff between Woods and Rocco Mediate, the hole was set up at 267 yards, giving players a chance to try to drive the green. And then there was the par-5 18th, which almost was converted to a par 4 but was left alone to add potential drama to the finish. The only hole with water on it, a small pond known as "Devlin's Billabong" that guards the front-left portion of the green, the home hole was played from forward tees to entice competitors to try to reach the putting surface in two.

16th
PAR 3
193/225 YARDS

The 16th hole, par 3 and 193 to 225 yards.

The 18th indeed would prove to be the pivotal hole of the championship, the one that saved eventual champion Woods not once but twice.

In the final analysis, Torrey Pines showed that it possessed more fight in it than usual to combat the skills of players in the modern era armed with the latest technology, with a 1-under-par aggregate score over 72 holes the best anyone could manage. The field averaged 74.725 on the par-71 arrangement.

Given the history of the property, that seemed more than appropriate. It should have put up a fight. After all, Torrey Pines Mesa once was more than 1,150 acres of barren land that became the ideal location first as a testing ground for aviator Charles Lindbergh, and later for the U.S. military to establish a base for would-be soldiers during World War II. At Camp Callan planes towed targets past the cliffs so soldiers could gain experience with their 90-millimeter anti-aircraft guns. The base's rifle range was located on what now are the South's second and fifth fairways. The main road cut through the heart of the property and manhole covers from that road can still be found on the South Course.

After the base closed following the war, the land went back to the city, and for a while automobile races were held on the plateau. Until 1956, the Torrey Pines Race Track offered a twisting 2.7-mile track that attracted top auto racers and motorcycle riders. City leaders then decided to put golf courses there, probably never envisioning that a course with an initial budget of just over $500,000 would one day receive a $3.5 million facelift and be the home of the national Open.

It would also turn out to be one of the most universally praised U.S. Open course setups despite its resistance to scoring, which Jones attributed to the redesigned putting surfaces.

"I think that the contours acted effectively like hazards," he said with noted pride in his voice. "The contours haven't allowed players to really go at pins and they make them tough to putt, too. There just aren't that many easy putts out there. In fact, there aren't many easy two-putts at these speeds they have them at. The other thing is the tongues and terraces where they have set the pins, they've been able to hide the holes behind the bunkers or near them and that has been a factor. All in all, we saw a course pretty generous tee to green, but not one anyone could really attack."

Not with clubs and not with criticism.

"I've always believed [the Open] should be a good, hard challenge," Luke Donald said. "And I think that the USGA is pretty good at finding tough courses and making them as tough as they can be. The course setup has been very good this year, very fair, and I think that that obviously helps make a great U.S. Open venue."

"I love the challenge of the way the USGA's got it set up," Davis Love III said. "It's obviously—I don't know the right way to put it, it's more fun to play than the last two years. There are some opportunities out there. If you hit good shots, you know you're going to get rewarded, and if you hit bad shots, you know that it's not the end of the world. And it's not such a fine line as the last two years."

"The USGA did the best job it's ever done in setting up a golf course," Mickelson said. "The way the course has been presented, it was the fairest, best test of golf. It gave the best players a chance to separate themselves. The mixture of tee boxes and movement of pin

17th
PAR 4
441 YARDS

placements was strategically the best it's ever been and really rewards great shotmaking as well as the ability to recover. It was really a great test."

Most of the credit, deservedly, went to Davis. Players singled him out for praise, and David Fay, executive director of the USGA, was equally complimentary, noting that the organization's blueprint was certainly adhered to in spirit if not to the letter.

"Mike does a very good job of jumping into the player's skin," Fay said. "While this is an elite athletic competition, it's also entertainment, and I applaud the effort because it gives fans and players something to talk about.

"Mike is a good player, and that could have been a negative because someone else might try to do more than should be done," Fay added. "But Mike doesn't fall into such a trap. When I say he does a good job of getting into the player's skin, that's at different levels, whether it's the U.S. Open or the U.S. Women's Amateur or a Junior Amateur. He is just very good with gauging what should be done with a golf course given the competition at hand, and this is one more example of that. He got it right, and we got it right."

18th
PAR 5
573 YARDS

The 18th hole, par 5 and 573 yards.

Rocco Mediate competed through two playoffs and a total of 128 holes, 37 in qualifying and 91 in the championship.

108th
U.S. OPEN
Qualifying

Pennsylvania native Rocco Mediate went from one playoff to another and almost won the 108th U.S. Open Championship.

The veteran PGA Tour player with five career victories found himself one of 11 men in the Columbus, Ohio, sectional vying in a playoff for seven spots in the championship after 36 holes at Brookside Golf & Country Club and Ohio State University's Scarlet Course. Mediate's second-round 67 tied him for 17th place at 5-under 139. He then birdied the first extra hole with a 4-foot putt to earn his 13th U.S. Open berth one year after suffering disappointment in the sectionals by losing a playoff and a chance to play in his home state at Oakmont Country Club, near Pittsburgh.

That the 45-year-old Mediate nearly won the title at Torrey Pines Golf Course, pushing No. 1 Tiger Woods to 19 playoff holes and 91 holes total, once again highlighted the importance of the qualifying process and the truly open nature of America's national golf championship.

A total of 8,390 entries were accepted, 92 percent of which were received via the Internet. There were 8,318 players who went through either one or both levels of qualifying for 84 spots that remained after 72 men were exempt into the 156-player field. The oldest applicant was Harris Moore Jr., age 79, from Los Angeles. Rico Hoey, age 12, of Rancho Cucamonga, Calif., was the youngest. Players came from all 50 states and from 69 countries.

Mediate advanced through the sectional most heavily attended by PGA Tour players one day after the completion of the Memorial Tournament in nearby Dublin, Ohio. In all, 23 spots were up for grabs among 140 players. Carl Pettersson, who would go on to tie for sixth place in the Open, was the medalist after 64-67–131. Pettersson and Mediate were among 17 players who competed in the Memorial Tournament.

Two other notable names advanced out of the Ohio sectional. One was former PGA champion Davis Love III, who saw his streak of 70 consecutive major championship starts end at the Masters. He shot 72-66–138 to qualify for his 18th straight U.S. Open. The other was Californian Pat Perez, who grew up in the San Diego area, and as a youth used to work at Torrey Pines and played there, he estimated, about 1,000 rounds. Perez, who also shot 138, was so keyed up that on the eve of the qualifier he said: "I won't even watch the Open if I don't make it." Like Love, he shot 138 and avoided the playoff.

Chris Stroud, of Netherland, Texas, finished tied for sixth in the Cordova, Tenn., qualifier that also had a fair share of PGA Tour players, and earned the distinction of advancing through both stages for the second year in a row. Justin Hicks and Jeff Wilson also made it through local and sectional qualifying for the second time. Hicks, another playoff survivor out of Columbus, first pulled off the local-sectional double in 2004. Wilson did it in 2000, where he ended up as low amateur at Pebble Beach Golf Links.

Chris Beljan, the 2002 USGA Junior Amateur champion from Mesa, Ariz., was among 36 qualifiers who went through both stages of qualifying, a number tied for the third highest total in championship history. Beljan, 23, shared medalist honors with former PGA champion Rich Beem at Shadow Hawk Golf Club in Richmond, Texas.

Players Who Were Fully Exempt for the 2008 U.S. Open (72)

Robert Allenby	9, 10, 17	Padraig Harrington	4, 9, 10, 11, 17	Justin Rose	8, 9, 10, 11, 17
Stuart Appleby	17	J.B. Holmes	17	Rory Sabbatini	9, 10, 17
Stephen Ames	8, 17	Charles Howell III	9, 10	Adam Scott	9, 10, 17
Woody Austin	9, 10, 17	Ryuji Imada	12	Vijay Singh	5, 9, 10, 12, 17
Aaron Baddeley	8, 9, 10, 17	Trevor Immelman	3, 17	Heath Slocum	9, 10
Brad Bryant	7	Lee Janzen	1, 8	Brandt Snedeker	9, 10, 17
Jonathan Byrd	10	Miguel Jimenez	14, 17	Henrik Stenson	11, 17
Angel Cabrera	1, 8, 11, 17	Zach Johnson	3, 9, 10, 17	Richard Sterne	11, 17
Mark Calcavecchia	9, 10	Robert Karlsson	17	Steve Stricker	8, 9, 10, 17
Michael Campbell	1	Martin Kaymer	17	Toru Taniguchi	15, 17
Paul Casey	8, 11, 17	Shingo Katayama	15, 17	*Michael Thompson	2
K.J. Choi	9, 10, 13, 17	Jerry Kelly	8	David Toms	8
Daniel Chopra	13	Anthony Kim	12, 17	Scott Verplank	8, 9, 10, 17
Stewart Cink	9, 10, 12, 17	Justin Leonard	17	Camilo Villegas	10
Tim Clark	9, 10, 17	Hunter Mahan	8, 9, 10, 17	Bubba Watson	8
Ben Curtis	4	Shaun Micheel	5	Boo Weekley	9, 10, 12, 17
Luke Donald	9, 17	Phil Mickelson	3, 5, 9, 10,	Mike Weir	17
Nick Dougherty	8, 11		12, 13, 17	Lee Westwood	11, 17
Ernie Els	9, 10, 11, 17	Colin Montgomerie	11	Brett Wetterich	9, 10
Niclas Fasth	8, 11, 17	Geoff Ogilvy	1, 9, 10, 12, 17	Oliver Wilson	14, 17
Steve Flesch	9, 13	**Sean O'Hair	17	Tiger Woods	1, 3, 4, 5, 8, 9,
Jim Furyk	1, 8, 9, 10, 17	Rod Pampling	17		10, 12, 13, 17
Sergio Garcia	6, 9, 10, 11, 12, 17	Ian Poulter	17		
Retief Goosen	1, 11, 17	Jeff Quinney	12, 17	*Amateur	
Todd Hamilton	4	John Rollins	9, 10	**Withdrew; replaced by qualifying	
Soren Hansen	11, 17	Andres Romero	11, 17	alternate Gary Wolstenholme	

Key to Player Exemptions:

1. Winners of the U.S. Open Championship for the last 10 years.
2. Winner of and runner-up in the 2007 U.S. Amateur Championship. (must be an amateur)
3. Winners of the Masters Tournament the last five years.
4. Winners of the British Open Championship the last five years.
5. Winners of the PGA of America Championship the last five years.
6. Winner of the 2008 Players Championship.
7. Winner of the 2007 U.S. Senior Open Championship.
8. From the 2007 U.S. Open Championship, the 15 lowest scorers and anyone tying for 15th place.
9. From the 2007 final official PGA Tour money list, the top 30 money leaders.
10. Those 30 players qualifying for the season-ending 2007 Tour Championship.
11. From the 2007 final official PGA European Tour money list, the top 15 money leaders.
12. From the 2008 official PGA Tour money list, the top 10 money leaders through May 26, 2008.
13. Any multiple winners of PGA Tour co-sponsored events whose victories are considered official from April 25, 2007 through June 1, 2008.
14. From the 2008 official PGA European Tour money list, the top two money leaders through May 26, 2008.
15. From the 2007 final official Japan Golf Tour money list, the top two money leaders provided they are within the top 75 point leaders of the World Golf Ranking at that time.
16. From the 2007 final official PGA Tour of Australasia money list, the top two money leaders provided they are within the top 75 point leaders of the World Golf Ranking at that time.
17. From the current World Golf Ranking list, the top 50 point leaders as of May 26, 2008.
18. Special exemptions selected by the USGA Executive Committee. International players not otherwise exempt as selected by the USGA Executive Committee.

Sectional Qualifying Results

Ibaraki Country Club
Osaka Pref., Japan
12 players for two spots

Craig Parry	70 - 68 – 138
Artemio Murakami	69 - 69 – 138

Lake Merced Golf Club
Daly City, Calif.
85 players for seven spots

John Ellis	69 - 71 – 140
Jason Gore	67 - 73 – 140
Michael Allen	70 - 70 – 140
Garrett Chaussard	68 - 73 – 141
Craig Barlow	71 - 70 – 141
*Jeff Wilson	70 - 71 – 141
*Jordan Cox	70 - 71 – 141

Ross Fisher

Alastair Forsyth

Jason Bohn

Thomas Levet

Craig Parry

Columbine Country Club
Littleton, Colo.
28 players for two spots

Brian Kortan	70 - 68 – 138
(P)Jay Choi	69 - 71 – 140

Walton Heath Golf Club
Surrey, England
42 players for seven spots

Ross Fisher	67 - 70 – 137
Alastair Forsyth	69 - 68 – 137
Ross McGowan	67 - 71 – 138
Robert Dinwiddie	71 - 67 – 138
Phillip Archer	69 - 69 – 138
(P) Thomas Levet	69 - 70 – 139
(P) Johan Edfors	69 - 70 – 139
(P)* **Gary Wolstenholme	68 - 71 – 139

Jupiter Hills Club (Hills Course)
Tequesta, Fla.
45 players for three spots

Bobby Collins	69 - 69 – 138
Philippe Gasnier	69 - 71 – 140
(P)Joey Lamielle	73 - 68 – 141

Matt Kuchar

Davis Love III

Mark O'Meara

Ansley Golf Club (Settingdown Creek Course)
Roswell, Ga.
37 players for three spots

Jason Bohn	62 - 67 – 129
Matt Kuchar	64 - 65 – 129
(P) D.J. Trahan	67 - 67 – 134

Conway Farms Golf Club
Lake Forest, Ill.
61 players for six spots

Hunter Haas	68 - 68 – 136
Chris Kirk	68 - 71 – 139
Ian Leggatt	69 - 70 – 139
D.A. Points	69 - 70 – 139
Mark O'Meara	70 - 70 – 140
(P) Jonathan Turcott	72 - 69 – 141

Boone Valley Golf Club
Augusta, Mo.
17 players for one spot

Bob Gaus	76 - 66 – 142

Nick Watney

Jesper Parnevik

OSU Golf Club (Scarlet Course) and Brookside Golf & Country Club
Columbus, Ohio
140 players for 23 spots

Carl Pettersson	64 - 67 – 131
Bart Bryant	69 - 65 – 134
Ben Crane	69 - 66 – 135
*Derek Fathauer	67 - 68 – 135
Joe Ogilvie	66 - 69 – 135
Robert Garrigus	63 - 72 – 135
*Kevin Tway	68 - 68 – 136
Dean Wilson	69 - 68 – 137
Fredrik Jacobson	71 - 66 – 137
Jarrod Lyle	69 - 68 – 137
John Mallinger	67 - 70 – 137
*Kyle Stanley	71 - 66 – 137
Nick Watney	66 - 71 – 137
Davis Love III	72 - 66 – 138
Jesper Parnevik	69 - 69 – 138
Pat Perez	71 - 67 – 138
(P) Rocco Mediate	72 - 67 – 139
(P) Chad Campbell	67 - 72 – 139
(P) Justin Hicks	69 - 70 – 139
(P) Steve Marino	69 - 70 – 139
(P) Dustin Johnson	70 - 69 – 139
(P) Eric Axley	70 - 69 – 139
(P) Jonathan Mills	73 - 66 – 139

Old Oaks Country Club
Purchase, N.Y.
65 players for four spots

Kevin Silva	70 - 69 – 139
Jeffrey Bors	72 - 70 – 142
Yohann Benson	75 - 67 – 142
(P) Mike Gilmore	70 - 73 – 143

Brett Quigley

Springfield Country Club
Columbus, Ohio
72 players for six spots

Peter Tomasulo	63 - 65 – 128
Andrew Dresser	67 - 66 – 133
Fernando Figueroa	67 - 67 – 134
Chris Devlin	68 - 67 – 135
Sean English	64 - 71 – 135
(P)*Jimmy Henderson	71 - 65 – 136

The Members Club at Four Streams
Beallsville, Md.
28 players for two spots

David Hearn	71 - 66 – 137
Brian Bergstol	71 - 68 – 139

Colonial Country Club and Chickasaw Country Club
Cordova, Tenn.
89 players for 14 spots

John Merrick	65 - 65 – 130
Scott Piercy	64 - 68 – 132
*Michael Quagliano	64 - 68 – 132
Brett Quigley	66 - 66 – 132
Kevin Streelman	64 - 69 – 133
Patrick Sheehan	66 - 68 – 134
Chris Stroud	65 - 69 – 134
Travis Bertoni	67 - 67 – 134
D.J. Brigman	64 - 70 – 134
Scott Sterling	66 - 70 – 136
Michael Letzig	68 - 68 – 136
Brandt Jobe	65 - 71 – 136
(P)Casey Wittenberg	69 - 68 – 137
(P)Mathew Goggin	67 - 70 – 137

Emerald Valley Golf Club
Creswell, Ore.
27 players for two spots

*Nick Taylor	70 - 68 – 138
Rob Rashell	69 - 71 – 140

Shadow Hawk Golf Club
Richmond, Texas
29 players for two spots

Rich Beem	67 - 70 – 137
Charlie Beljan	69 - 70 – 139

*Denotes amateur   (P) Won playoff

**Qualified when exempt player Sean O'Hair withdrew

Casey Wittenberg

Bobby Collins

Rich Beem

Patrick Sheehan

No. 1 Tiger Woods was in a featured group with No. 3 Adam Scott (left) and No. 2 Phil Mickelson (right).

108th
U.S. OPEN
First Round

Tiger Woods is used to being the center of attention, the eye of the storm, the global icon whose mantra is: "I can." But when the 108th U.S. Open Championship commenced on June 12 at Torrey Pines Golf Course in San Diego, the spotlight on the No. 1 player in the world was more intense perhaps than ever before.

The world had not seen Woods in competition since early April in Augusta, Ga., when he finished second in the Masters Tournament to Trevor Immelman. Woods had begun the year talking about the acquisition of the Grand Slam—winning all four major championships in one year—and how it was "easily within reason," an assessment that was as honest as it was plausible, given his impeccable form at the end of the 2007 season. He had four wins in his last five events, including the PGA Championship, and he already had won four majors in a row over the 2000-01 seasons.

But two days after his second straight runner-up finish at Augusta National Golf Club, Woods underwent arthroscopic surgery on his left knee to repair cartilage damage. He was forced to skip the Wachovia Championship, at which he was the defending champion, and The Players Championship. But he had planned all along since the day of the operation—his third on the knee—to return to tournament golf at the Memorial Tournament to help him prepare for the U.S. Open at Torrey Pines' South Course, a layout where he had enjoyed immense success dating back to his junior golf days.

He never got to Muirfield Village Golf Club and Jack Nicklaus' invitational tournament in suburban Columbus, Ohio. He simply wasn't healthy enough to play a round of golf.

Would he be ready for the Open? Would he be able to walk 18 holes a day (which he hadn't been able to do since the surgery), let alone hit golf shots? Would he be able to exhibit a level of skill and proficiency necessary to navigate a familiar but fortified course, one infused with all the United States Golf Association features—firm, fast greens, narrowed fairways, penal rough—and somehow vie for his third U.S. Open crown?

These were the primary questions in the days leading up to the championship. For all the talk of the local favorite, 37-year-old Phil Mickelson, having a chance to win his first U.S. Open on the course he played as a boy, the central storyline was still Woods, age 32, and his health and just how prepared he would be for the year's second major championship.

Some golf aficionados tried to compare his layoff to one he took in 2006 prior to the Open after his father, Earl, passed away in early May.

"A couple of years ago when dad passed it was … coming back and playing was a lot more difficult than I thought, just because everything I did … if I take time off and I come back, I always work on my fundamentals. Well, who taught me my fundamentals? It was dad," Woods explained to a full contingent of media personnel two days before the start of the championship.

"All the things I had to go through and my preparation for tournaments, my dad taught me all those things. Overcoming and getting out and playing and practicing, I didn't want to do that because I'd always think about dad. That was the hardest thing. Usually people go to work to get away from it. But to me it brought more feelings

D.A. Points (74) was first off—and made a birdie.

Despite two double bogeys, Woods (72) was near the top.

out when I came to work. So it was a little more difficult practicing and preparing.

"This [week] is totally different, going through having a procedure done right after the Masters and now here, you can't compare the two mentally, they're two totally different places."

Of course, his father had always tried to prepare him to be the most mentally impervious competitor, and Woods had to call on all his powers of concentration and psychological resourcefulness to gird for the first two rounds of the championship, which he would share with Mickelson and Adam Scott in an unprecedented grouping of the top three players in the Official World Golf Ranking. The USGA had decided for the first time to send the top 12 players in the world off in four sets of threes, meaning players ranked 4-6, 7-9 and 10-12 also would compete alongside one another.

Adding further intrigue to the gathering of the top trio was the fact that Scott was not in top physical form either, having broken a bone on the outside of his right hand prior to the Memorial Tournament. Mickelson undoubtedly must have been feeling pangs of empathy, having competed in the 2007 U.S. Open at Oakmont Country Club wearing a brace on his wrist, which he had injured preparing for that particularly harsh Open assignment.

The three were slated to tee off on the par-4 first hole at Torrey South at 8:06 a.m. PDT, but the electricity surging throughout the grounds of the municipal facility began hours earlier and almost could have lit up San Diego County. Spectators were lined up 18-20 deep around the first tee box to see the opening shots, while all down the length of the fairway at the 448-yard par-4 hole, people crowded the gallery ropes at least six deep.

Shouts of "Phil" and "Tiger" permeated the air in rifle-like succession as each man stepped on

Kevin Streelman (68) once shared the lead in the 2008 Buick Invitational and was paired with Tiger Woods.

the tee box amid the misty coastal air known as "June Gloom." Mickelson was the first to arrive at exactly 8 a.m., and when he stood and folded his tee sheet at the starter's podium where the USGA's Ron Read was stationed to announce each player in the championship before he teed off, fans start yelling, "Speech! Speech!"

When Mickelson pretended to say a few words into the microphone, the crowd erupted in cheers and laughter.

Scott was next to arrive at 8:03 a.m., and the applause was polite, but without accompanying vocal acoustics. Woods was right on the Australian's heels, and a surge of yelling, cheering and clapping ensued. The two-time U.S. Open champion extended his right hand to shake the hand of Scott, but instead he received the Aussie's left hand.

"I don't even want to know how you did that," Woods said to him while smiling.

Rocco Mediate (69) tied for sixth in his last event.

Stuart Appleby (69) hit from the third tee, on the scenic coastal bluffs at Torrey Pines.

Eric Axley (69) aimed to make the cut.

"Ask me no questions and I'll tell you no lies," Scott responded with a grin.

That was about it for the smiling in the group, as teeth clenching ensued. Woods had worried aloud about his ability to start out decently in the championship, and had said that his problems at Winged Foot were the result of taking three to four holes to truly get into the flow of the round. "I was always playing catch-up," he explained.

And he found himself doing so again at Torrey Pines, making a double-bogey 6 at the first hole for his first double bogey in 416 holes. Woods drove into heavy rough left of the fairway bunker, chopped out and then knocked his wedge shot over the green. A chip to 5 feet out of a thick lie and two putts, and it seemed like 2006 all over again. Woods, with a bit of charm, later would disagree.

"Getting into the flow of the round it helps when you hit six shots on the first hole to get into the flow," he said. "That's a lot of shots to get into a flow."

Interjecting a few grimaces between golf swings, Woods was not sharp, as expected, but neither did he crumble, and at the end of the day, he

First Round

Justin Hicks	68	-3
Kevin Streelman	68	-3
Rocco Mediate	69	-2
Stuart Appleby	69	-2
Eric Axley	69	-2
Geoff Ogilvy	69	-2
*Rickie Fowler	70	-1
Robert Karlsson	70	-1
Lee Westwood	70	-1
Robert Allenby	70	-1
Ernie Els	70	-1

*Denotes amateur

Vijay Singh (71) had a promising start.

carded a 1-over-par 72 and was right in the mix. "To make two double bogeys and a three-putt and only be four back, that's a great position to be in, because I know I can clean that up tomorrow," Woods said.

Mickelson, after his 71, and Scott, who shot 73, had cleaning up to do, too. Mickelson, a four-time U.S. Open runner-up, also had some explaining to do.

A former Junior World champion and three-time winner of the Buick Invitational, Mickelson couldn't have been more excited to be playing in the national championship at this hometown course. Other than Woods and Pat Perez, who as a boy used to work a variety of jobs at the public facility, no one knew or understood the nuances of the South Course better than Mickelson. So when he showed up on the first tee without a driver in his bag—just two years after winning his second Masters title by using two drivers—there were raised eyebrows and, afterward, a few raised questions, even after he reached both par-5 holes on the inward nine in two shots and converted birdies at both. Alas, he managed to find just six fairways all day, which thwarted his momentum.

"You noticed that I didn't have a driver today, huh?" Mickelson said, grinning. "My game plan was that I only want to hit it a certain distance, I don't really want to hit it past 300 yards on most of the par 4s because it starts running into the rough.

Bob Tway caddied for his son, amateur Kevin (75).

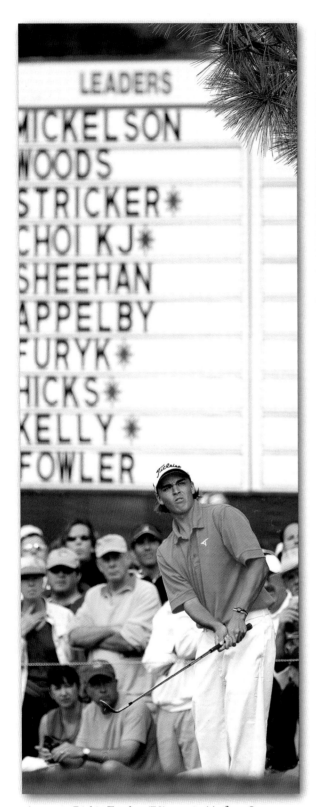

LEADERS
MICKELSON
WOODS
STRICKER*
CHOI KJ*
SHEEHAN
APPELBY
FURYK*
HICKS*
KELLY*
FOWLER

Amateur Rickie Fowler (70) was in his first Open.

Robert Allenby (70) was off to his best Open start.

And I felt like with the fairways being firm like they were today, all I needed was a 3-wood on the holes.

But he noted that his inability to hit more fairways, "kind of defeats the game plan, because now I'm short and crooked."

Scott was perhaps even less prepared than Woods after breaking his hand in a car door while in London. Had he not been a practitioner of the overlapping grip, he insisted he wouldn't have been able to play. Despite the handicap, he hung in there, perhaps because of the company he was keeping.

"I know it's a big pairing and there's a lot of hoopla about it, but often when I played with, I played with Phil a lot in majors, it seems like I get drawn with him a lot. But I enjoy playing with Tiger as well," the 27-year-old Australian said. "I find it a lot easier to focus because I think I've got to be a little more disciplined. And I felt like I played really well out there today and I really didn't make any putts. So my game didn't feel too bad."

While the Nuevo Big Three were slashing at Torrey South, a familiar Open storyline was developing at the top of the leaderboard with the emergence of two relatively unknown players, Kevin Streelman and Justin Hicks, claiming first place at 3-under 68 for a one-shot lead over four more well-known players. The two men, neither among the top 600 in the World Ranking, were among 11 who broke par at Torrey Pines.

Streelman, age 29, didn't seem intimidated, and perhaps for good reason. Earlier in the year, the PGA Tour rookie had been paired with Woods on the weekend at Torrey Pines during the Buick Invitational, which Woods would go on to win for a fourth straight year and sixth time overall. Streelman ended up tied for 29th at the Buick Invitational after shooting 75-77 on the weekend, but he seemed to have found his return to the South Course an uplifting experience.

"It's been an incredible run on the PGA Tour thus far," said Streelman, who also had a pretty busy couple of weeks leading into the championship, qualifying in the Tennessee sectional and then getting married in Naples, Fla. "I don't think what happened today has quite sunk in.

"There was definitely a familiarity effect," he added. "I love a lot of the tee shots out here. I feel the course is set up perfectly for a U.S. Open, very fair. You have abilities to make birdies. You're probably not going to make a bunch of them, but if you hit balls in the right spots, you can save pars. And if you hit great shots, you're rewarded with good birdie looks."

While some fans might have recognized Streelman, Hicks, playing in his second U.S. Open, had to explain his odd case of mistaken identity. There was a player named Justin Hicks who competed in the Buick Invitational in January, but that was a club professional from San Diego. The Justin Hicks, age 33, who occupied the top spot with Streelman was a member of the Nationwide Tour who had never competed in a professional event at Torrey Pines.

The local Justin Hicks came out to watch the other Justin Hicks during the opening round and saw him cover the opening nine holes in six under par before he gave a few shots back. There was no talk of trading places. That had been happening enough.

"The [PGA] Tour got us mixed up, companies got us mixed up," the U.S. Open-playing Hicks explained. [His] checks were going to my place,

Robert Karlsson (70) played the second nine in 33.

Justin Hicks (68) had seven birdies in his round.

Defending champion Angel Cabrera (79) went out in 43.

Phil Mickelson (71) played without his driver.

[my] checks were going to his place. They actually withdrew me out of the Nationwide Tour event. I called them up and they said, 'You committed to the Buick Invitational, and we figured you wouldn't want to go to Panama.' I said, 'No, I'd like to go to Panama because that's not me.'"

Of course, a lot of players ended up not performing like themselves, at least not of late.

The four men tied for third place were 2006 U.S. Open winner Geoff Ogilvy, Stuart Appleby, Rocco Mediate and left-hander Eric Axley. Mediate had missed eight cuts in 17 PGA Tour starts before the Open, though he showed signs of life at the Memorial Tournament in rallying for a tie for sixth place.

Ogilvy, playing in his fifth U.S. Open, broke par for the first time. "I'm playing pretty well," said Ogilvy, who rallied after bogeys at two of the first three holes to put himself in the top 10 after the first round for the third straight year. "I played really well at Colonial, Memorial, without playing great. It was just nice. I'm hitting it decently and putting okay, just a putt or two away from being right there at the end, at the end of the week."

One of Ogilvy's playing companions, two-time U.S. Open champion Ernie Els, gave two shots back at the end of the round, but he was among five players who shot 70. The others were Robert Allenby,

Geoff Ogilvy (69) finally broke par in the Open.

Lee Westwood, Robert Karlsson and 19-year-old amateur Rickie Fowler.

Els, who just missed out on the top pairing with Woods and Mickelson when he dropped in the World Ranking after the Memorial Tournament, recorded his first sub-par score in the Open since 2004. He was encouraged after missing four of his last six cuts.

"I haven't broken par since TPC (The Players), so I must be doing something right," Els said. "Obviously I would have taken anything around par, even today, anything not too bad. Under par today, you know, is a great score for me. I really felt very comfortable with my swing."

Not everyone could say the same thing. Defending champion Angel Cabrera, who had quit smoking in the months before the U.S. Open, didn't make a birdie until the 13th hole and shot 79. Immelman, the Masters champion, shot 75. Sergio Garcia, the winner of The Players Championship, suffered a double bogey at the first hole, like Woods, on the way to 76, joining two-time U.S. Open champion Retief Goosen. British Open champion Padraig Harrington had 78. Twenty players failed to break 80, and one other, Mark Calcavecchia, withdrew.

No one failed to notice that Woods was within striking distance of those at the top of the leaderboard, almost like he had never been gone.

Ernie Els (70) dropped two shots in his last five holes.

Lee Westwood (70) parred his final nine holes.

Stuart Appleby (139) acknowledged his 45-foot birdie putt on the 18th for 1-under 70 and the 36-hole lead.

Australia's Stuart Appleby might have seized the lead after 36 holes of the 108th U.S. Open Championship, but Tiger Woods seized the moment and the momentum and captivated witnesses the world over with one of the most astounding performances of a career filled with countless efforts of similar high quality and high drama.

Playing alongside Phil Mickelson and Adam Scott again in the championship's featured grouping, Woods, the No. 1 player in the world, put on a putting clinic at the South Course at Torrey Pines to put to rest any lingering notions of whether he or his game were healthy enough to challenge for the national title. An inward 5-under-par 30 achieved by sinking a series of medium-length putts gave Woods a 3-under-par 68 and 2-under 140 total, just one stroke off the pace set by Appleby, whose 70 left him alone in front at 139, his first lead in a U.S. Open and the eighth 36-hole lead of his career.

Wearing a green shirt, looking for red numbers and leaving his playing partners in the dust near dusk, Woods birdied four of five holes in a dash that was as surprising as it was mesmerizing. Beginning his second round at the 10th hole, Woods opened with a bogey, and he turned in 38. But taking advantage of a fortunate break after a wayward drive at the first hole, Woods fist-pumped his way into a tie for second with Rocco Mediate and Robert Karlsson.

"I didn't do anything. I actually just kept patient," Woods explained after another round filled not only with great shots but shooting pain in his surgically repaired left leg that had him winc-

ing and, at times, looking worried. "I was trying to get back to even par for the tournament. I was playing the back nine at even par. All of a sudden they started flying in from everywhere.

"If I shot three under par on that back nine, that would put me at even par for the tournament. And I just got a couple more."

For the second day in a row, Woods began his round ingloriously, three-putting the 10th hole for a bogey—after ending his first round Thursday with a three-putt par. He also bogeyed the 12th, got the two shots back in a hurry with a 15-foot eagle putt at the 599-yard par-5 13th, and then, inexplicably, bogeyed twice more and failed to birdie the par-5 18th, a hole that in his career he has never made worse than par.

When he pushed his drive far to the right at the par-4 first hole, he appeared to be in peril of seeing his round spiral out of control. His ball, however, came to rest near a tree on a trampled down bare lie next to the cart path. He opted not to take a free drop, because it would have put him behind the tree. Wearing metal spikes, he then had to make a careful swing with his 8-iron while standing on the cart path. His shot from 157 yards settled to 10 feet, and he drained the putt. That bit of luck and better skill on the recovery literally kick-started his rally.

"I made some 15- and 20-foot putts and got on a roll that way," said Woods, who converted birdies at the second, fourth, fifth and ninth holes, all from 18 feet or longer except at the last, which was a mere tap-in after reaching the green in two. "Whether you call it the zone or not, it just feels it's a nice rhythm. Been there before. I've shot some good rounds doing that.

Saving par at the 11th, Rocco Mediate (140) shot even-par 71 to be one stroke out of the lead.

Robert Karlsson (140) began with a pair of 70s.

"You're just at the halfway point," added Woods, who trailed after 36 holes in 30 of his 64 victories on the PGA Tour. "You're just trying to play and position yourself. This golf course is only going to get harder and more difficult. It can bite you in a hurry."

His playing companions knew that only too well.

Mickelson, who shot 75, and Scott, who shot a second straight 73, had their moments, too, but mostly they got stuck in neutral and were reduced to spectators almost blending into the huge galleries as Woods summoned his Torrey Pines magic. They combined for just four birdies, and each man bogeyed a par-5 hole. When Woods began to surge ahead, the No. 2 and 3 players in the world seemed to be caught off guard and then got off stride.

The former, in particular, appeared to be feeling each fist pump that Woods let fly, like they were literally punching him in the gut. Mickelson, pointing toward this U.S. Open in his back-

Second Round

Stuart Appleby	69 - 70	– 139	-3
Rocco Mediate	69 - 71	– 140	-2
Robert Karlsson	70 - 70	– 140	-2
Tiger Woods	72 - 68	– 140	-2
D.J. Trahan	72 - 69	– 141	-1
Davis Love III	72 - 69	– 141	-1
Lee Westwood	70 - 71	– 141	-1
Miguel Angel Jimenez	75 - 66	– 141	-1
Luke Donald	71 - 71	– 142	E
Robert Allenby	70 - 72	– 142	E
Geoff Ogilvy	69 - 73	– 142	E
Ernie Els	70 - 72	– 142	E
Carl Pettersson	71 – 71	– 142	E

Tiger Woods (140) had four birdies in five holes.

yard, was hoping to close the Open wound of four runner-up finishes. He left himself in a dyspeptic position, seven behind Appleby and six behind Woods.

"I didn't get anything going," said Mickelson, who again left his driver at home but still hit just six fairways, the same as in the first round. "I made some good pars. But when I made a birdie I followed it with a bogey. And I didn't get the momentum out of the round. I was just fighting. I was fighting to stay in it. It hurt to finish with two bogeys.

"I'm at four over, and I'm going to come back tomorrow and try to get this thing back to even par and should have a chance on the weekend."

While every stroke that Woods executed brought increasing amounts of intrigue to the proceedings, Appleby needed just one "sweet" shot to execute the hopes of nearly a dozen players. His 45-foot birdie putt at the par-5 18th hole knocked out 11 players, including 2007 Masters champion Zach Johnson, who were clinging to a life preserver known as the 10-shot rule. All players within 10 shots of the leader in the U.S. Open make the 36-hole cut. So, when Appleby snuck in at 3-under 139, all players at eight over par were sent packing.

Johnson, who birdied his last hole, was disappointed, but weightier issues were mostly the cause of his subdued demeanor. Early Friday he watched

D.J. Trahan (141) was enjoying more than he expected.

on the news as downtown Cedar Rapids, Iowa, where he grew up and where his dad, a chiropractor, has an office, was flooded by the overflowing Cedar River. "It was definitely hard to concentrate," he said. "I mean, there's a reality check right there."

Also missing the cut were two of the last three U.S. Open winners in Angel Cabrera, the defending champion, and Michael Campbell, the 2005 winner. Cabrera added a 5-over 76 to his ugly opening 79 to end up 13 over par. Campbell ballooned to a second-round 83 to tumble to 19-over-par 161. And two-time champion Lee Janzen, qualifying via the last year of his 10-year exemption for win-

ning the 1998 Open at The Olympic Club, hit the flagstick with his opening approach on his opening hole Thursday, but he had few other highlights in rounds of 75-78–153.

In all, 80 of the 156 players advanced to play the weekend with scores of 149 or better, including Ireland's Padraig Harrington, the reigning British Open champion, who rallied from an opening 78 with a 4-under 67, the second best round of the day. Masters winner Trevor Immelman, who won the 1998 U.S. Amateur Public Links Championship at Torrey Pines, kept his hopes alive for the Grand Slam by carding 73–148. Sergio Garcia, winner of The Players Championship and among the pre-championship favorites, fired a 1-under 70 to come in at 146. Garcia had begun six over par after seven holes before playing the next 29 holes in two under par.

Former major championship winners Todd Hamilton and Rich Beem made their first cuts in the U.S. Open. Hamilton was making his sixth start in the Open and Beem his seventh. Both carded 74–148.

First-round co-leaders Kevin Streelman and Justin Hicks fell back to Earth, but they didn't fall out of the championship. Streelman suffered a triple bogey at the par-3 third hole on the way to a 6-over 77 and 145 total. Hicks tumbled to 80 to get in the house at 148, the only player in the field to fail to break 80 in the second round and still make the cut.

"If Thursday morning I would have said three over at a U.S. Open through two rounds, I would

Despite this bogey at the 15th hole, Lee Westwood (141) finished with 71, even par in the second round.

have taken it," said Streelman, one of 16 first-time Open participants to make the cut. "I'm a little disappointed how I played today, but, hopefully, it's my bad round and I'll make a move tomorrow."

Three amateurs, all still in college, also survived—Derek Fathauer, Rickie Fowler, the Ben Hogan Award winner as the top collegiate player, and U.S. Amateur runner-up Michael Thompson—the first time in three years an amateur qualified for the weekend. Fathauer and Thompson each shot 73 for 146 and 147 totals, respectively. Fowler added 79 to 70 for 149, making it on the number.

Woods wasn't the only member of the walking wounded who occupied a prime spot on the leaderboard. Mediate, with his famously fragile back, remained near the top with an even-par 71 that left him in a tie for second with Woods and Karlsson at 2-under 140, one stroke behind Appleby. Karlsson, from Sweden, carded his second straight 70. Davis Love III, sidelined last autumn by a torn tendon in his left ankle that eventually required surgery, fired 69 for a 1-under 141 total. Love was tied for fifth place with Spain's Miguel Angel Jimenez,

Miguel Angel Jimenez (141) shot 66, the day's best.

Ernie Els (142) was out front with the leaders, here hitting his approach shot to the fifth green.

Luke Donald (142) had two even-par 71s.

who carded the low round of the day, a 5-under 66, England's Lee Westwood, who shot 71, and D.J. Trahan, a former U.S. Amateur Public Links champion, who shot 69.

Just eight men remained in red under-par figures at the halfway mark. Another five were at even-par 142, including England's Luke Donald, who shot his second 71, and Australians Robert Allenby and 2006 U.S. Open champion Geoff Ogilvy, who posted 72 and 73 respectively. Two-time U.S. Open winner Ernie Els, from South Africa, also landed at level par after shooting 72, as did Sweden's Carl Pettersson with his two 71s.

While Mediate, whose back acted up in mid-round enough to require him to ingest a few pain relievers, might have been a surprise in lingering near the top, Love was an afterthought until he

Robert Allenby (142) was one under on his last 13 holes.

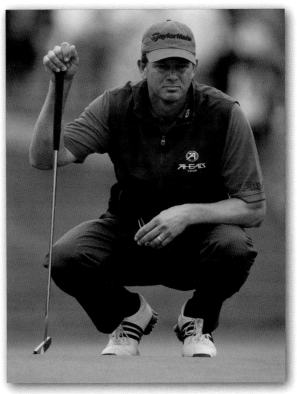

Retief Goosen (145) recovered with 69.

popped up with his best round in the U.S. Open since his final-round 69 in 2005 that lifted him into a tie for sixth at Pinehurst's No. 2 Course in his native North Carolina.

Playing in his 20th Open, Love, age 44, had missed the Masters to sit out of a major championship after 70 straight appearances dating back to the 1990 British Open. While excited about his performance, which included a series of clutch pars—or "Open pars," as he called them—Love was still smarting over his absence from Augusta. "If I win the U.S. Open, it doesn't make up for missing the Masters," said Love, who in recent years also had been battling neck and back problems.

"I know the year (1988) my daughter was born I did have to qualify [for the U.S. Open] … and she just turned 20," said Love, the 1997 PGA Championship winner. "I wish the Masters had 36-hole qualifying, because I think I could have made it through."

Mediate knows about missed chances at the Masters, too. In 2006 he sat in fourth place after

Davis Love III (141) shot 33 on his second nine.

Jim Furyk (145) posted 71 to bounce back.

Steve Stricker (149) shot 76, on the cut line.

Padrig Harrington (145) came in with 67, four under.

54 holes, but his back gave out and his final-round 80 dropped him back to a tie for 37th place. He was feeling better at Torrey Pines, where he hadn't had much success—but, of course, it hadn't been set up like a U.S. Open before.

"I feel absolutely perfect," Mediate said. "I have no problems. Is there any wood up here? I have no problems. I love this type of golf. This golf course is set up so nice, it's good. But it's my favorite tournament. It's great. You know, I don't have many mornings left. I'm in a great spot. We'll see what happens."

Appleby, age 37, nearly won the Masters in 2007, leading after three rounds before falling back to seventh place. An eight-time winner on the PGA Tour, he also lost to Els in a four-man play-off in the 2002 British Open. For the most part, though, he hasn't gotten on well with major championships, recording just four top-10s in 45 appear-

As spectators watched from the branches, Adam Scott (146) took bogey from beneath a tree at the 18th, his ninth hole.

ances. Meanwhile, he came in with 18 missed cuts in Grand Slam events.

"Majors are not a comfort zone," said Appleby, whose tie for 10th in 1998 at The Olympic Club was his only top-10 finish in the U.S. Open and, in fact, the only time he had been in the top 10 after any round before taking the lead at Torrey Pines. "They're not supposed to be comfortable. That's sort of why there's only four of them a year, and they're always on testing golf courses.

"Do I think that I am more comfortable? Yeah, I guess I might be. I think as you get older, you've got to find a way to be more comfortable in positions always trying to put you off balance. Is there a physical skill out here? For sure, in a U.S. Open. There's a lot of mental skill, too. And that's probably the one that you're trying to control the most. I guess effectively by trying to gain control out here, you've got to let go of control. And that is not a natural thing to do. That's why it's so difficult."

With Woods letting go with his barrage, no one was feeling comfortable. Appleby didn't seem inclined to move out of Woods' way on the golf course, but as he completed his post-round press conference, the No. 1 player in the world stepped into the room, and Appleby quickly took the cue that his time at the podium had expired.

"I can go now. Tiger's here," he said with a smile. Then he directed a question at Woods. "You're all finished, right?"

Woods nodded. He was finished, at least for the time being.

"He wants to go play golf, we want to go play golf," said Appleby, who is a Florida neighbor of Woods at the Isleworth residential community southwest of Orlando. "And I'll be throwing a club toward his sore knee. It would be an accident, of course."

After his putt on the 18th for eagle, Tiger Woods (210) demonstrated with a slow fist pump and a wide grin.

I t was sloppy and shaky, serendipitous and sweet, scintillating and, at the very end, oh, so satisfying. Everyone could see how satisfying it was. The Cheshire cat grin gave that away, the one he couldn't hide as he slowly but emphatically pumped his right fist after his final stroke of the day tracked perfectly into the hole.

Tiger Woods never seems to run out of encores. Or escapes. Or ways to change the conversation, for that matter.

England's Lee Westwood was safely in the media center at Torrey Pines Golf Course with the third-round lead in the 108th U.S. Open Championship after he shot a 1-under-par 70 on the South Course for a 2-under 211 total. Woods was two strokes behind and still struggling with his aching knee and in trouble again at the 17th hole when Westwood finished. But in a matter of minutes the questions that members of the media contingent directed at Westwood had changed from talking about his lead and his chance to end Europe's 38-year drought in the U.S. Open to how he would try to overtake Woods in the championship's final round.

Huh?

Yes, it was just that swift and stunning. First, Woods didn't just extricate himself from a scruffy lie in the greenside rough on Torrey South's 17th hole, he popped it in the hole for an unlikely birdie. The 18th was much more predictable and familiar. A good drive and a 5-wood set up a downhill 40-foot putt for eagle, his second in a five-hole span. The ball went down, his fist went up, the immense throng went wild and the hopes of Westwood and the rest of the competition went into a tailspin.

Recovering from a five-shot deficit over his final six holes, Woods snuck in under par, with a 1-under 70, and posted 3-under 210 total for a one-shot lead through 54 holes. With a perfect mark in 13 opportunities playing from such a position in the major championships, Woods ended up in the place he likes more than any other and with which he is most comfortable even on the day when it appeared unlikely he could get there.

He struggled with his driver and the soreness in his left leg and still managed to post one of the 11 sub-par rounds on an afternoon when the ocean mists wouldn't relinquish their hold over the picturesque landscape.

"That's what it's all about is getting the ball in the hole in as few shots as possible," Woods said after his remarkable closing run Saturday, the second day in a row in which he had been able to find another gear and initiate a kick to the finish. "I was just trying to manage my game, stay in there. It's a U.S. Open; guys are not going to go low. Even though I got off to such a poor start again, I just hung around. I was just trying to get back to even par, either for the tournament or for the day. The day would be great. But even if I finished at even par for the tournament, it wouldn't be a bad thing either.

"And then, all of a sudden, things started turning."

They always seem to for the No. 1 player in the world. That left everyone else seemingly vying for second place. Westwood, who knew full well that countryman Tony Jacklin in 1970 was the last European to capture the U.S. Open, was one stroke back, while Rocco Mediate, who at one point in the

Phil Mickelson (222) fell 12 strokes behind.

middle of the round held a three-stroke lead, was the last of the three players under par after 72 left him at 1-under 212. Australia's Geoff Ogilvy also posted 72 and America's D.J. Trahan shot 73 and both were at 1-over 214.

There were five more players tied at 2-over 215, rounding out the top-10 leaders: America's Hunter Mahan, who shot 69, and Colombia's Camilo Villegas, Australia's Robert Allenby, Spain's Miguel Angel Jimenez and Sweden's Robert Karlsson.

In another strong group at 3-over 216 were two-time U.S. Open champion Ernie Els of South Africa, Spain's Sergio Garcia, Canada's Mike Weir and America's John Merrick.

No one else was closer than six shots. That included the sentimental hometown choice, Phil Mickelson, who had hoped to whittle his way back toward even par for the championship. Instead, he blew himself out of contention when he suffered a quadruple-bogey 9 at the par-5 13th hole, carded 76 and dropped to 222, tied for 47th place, nine over par for the week.

By putting a driver in his golf bag for the first time, Mickelson had changed his game plan, and he tried to be more aggressive. But his swing, which he had been trying to shore up for more than a year with his coach, Butch Harmon, simply wasn't cooperating. He double-crossed himself with clubs as short as an 8-iron, and he continued to miss fairways. Lefty found just six fairways on Saturday and his 18 total through three rounds ranked last among the 80 players who made the cut.

Nevertheless, Mickelson couldn't blame his driver alone for the unfortunate mess he made of the reachable 13th. He had come to the hole still just one over par for the day. Three weeks before the Open, Mickelson had won the Crowne Plaza Invitational at Colonial with five wedges in his bag, and all he needed was one good one to help him at the 13th hole. After laying up to 80 yards in two, Mickelson tried to get too cute with an L-wedge to stick it close to the front hole location. The ball spun off the green and down the slope nearly back to his feet. He switched to his 64-degree wedge, but that didn't help. Three more shots were required before

Stuart Appleby (218) shot 79 after going out in 41.

Trevor Immelman (220) enjoyed Masters prominence.

the ball stayed on the putting surface. Three putts later, he had the 9.

"I've had a 9 on 13 [before]," Mickelson said bravely afterward. "I was 8 years old, but I have had a 9 there."

Even with the Open lost, he hadn't lost his sense of humor. But the disappointment of the week clearly hurt.

"This is something I wanted a lot and I just haven't played well this week," said Mickelson, a four-time Open runner-up. "I think it's an exciting Open. I'm certainly disappointed that I'm not in the mix right now. That was the goal. So I'm going to come out tomorrow and enjoy my final round."

Woods wasn't much enjoying his third round. The day appeared to belong to others, most notably Mediate, who was playing in the final group with second-round leader Stuart Appleby. While Appleby shot 41 on his first nine—which included a four-putt double bogey at the fifth and a three-putt bogey at the ninth—on his way to 79 for a

Brandt Jobe (217) shared 15th place after his 69.

On the 13th hole, Woods holed a double-breaking, 70-foot putt for eagle 3.

Miguel Angel Jimenez (215) fell back with 74.

tie for 19th at 218, Mediate went out in 34 with birdies at the second and fifth holes offsetting his bogey at the third. When he birdied the 10th hole from 8 feet after hitting a "cut pitching wedge," he was four under par and three shots clear of the field.

Westwood was hanging in, but Woods was showing his human side. He again made double bogey at the par-4 first hole on the way to an outward 37 and found himself five strokes behind Mediate when he bogeyed the long par-4 12th. Things looked even bleaker when his drive at the 13th sailed way right. After taking a free drop for line-of-sight relief, he blistered a 5-iron from 210 yards that he was merely hoping would, at worst, end up in the back bunker. Instead, it checked up on the back of the green, nearly 70 feet from the hole.

No player has a better feel and understanding of the greens at Torrey Pines than Woods does. In

Third Round

Tiger Woods	72 - 68 - 70 – 210	-3
Lee Westwood	70 - 71 - 70 – 211	-2
Rocco Mediate	69 - 71 - 72 – 212	-1
Geoff Ogilvy	69 - 73 - 72 – 214	+1
D.J. Trahan	72 - 69 - 73 – 214	+1
Hunter Mahan	72 - 74 - 69 – 215	+2
Camilo Villegas	73 - 71 - 71 – 215	+2
Robert Allenby	70 - 72 - 73 – 215	+2
Miguel Angel Jimenez	75 - 66 - 74 – 215	+2
Robert Karlsson	70 - 70 - 75 – 215	+2

Lee Westwood (211) was leading when he finished.

fact, no player can match his touch at any venue, but the mental cartography he was able to call upon from all the great rounds at Torrey Pines surely helped him with the eagle putt at the 13th. The double-breaker tracked slowly toward the hole and then veered sharply left and in.

"The antics, I saw it all," said Mediate, who had been standing back in the fairway and watched the putt careen into the hole. "Completely out of his mind. The stuff he does is unreal."

Mediate, perhaps shaken a bit, bogeyed the hole, but Woods gave the stroke back at the 14th after a wild drive cost him another bogey. At the 15th, Woods produced yet another poor swing, and he nearly fell on the follow through. He lingered on the tee box for a few anxious seconds before carrying on.

"I just keep telling myself that if it grabs me and if I get that shooting pain, I get it, but it's always after impact, so go ahead and just make the proper swing if I can," Woods said. "But if pain hits, pain hits. So be it. It's just pain."

Just pain. Perhaps it's easier to take when you've been dishing it out for more than a decade.

Woods managed to save par at the 15th and then again at the 232-yard par-3 16th with a nifty up and down. When he drove again into the rough at the 17th, his face showed a combination of frustration and fatigue. On the range before the round he had been trying to decipher the cause of a two-way miss—when he didn't know if a poor shot would go right or left. That carried over to the round.

Rocco Mediate (212) took double-bogey 6 at the 15th.

Camilo Villegas (215) shot a second 71.

Sergio Garcia (216) followed 76 with two 70s.

Geoff Ogilvy (214) shared fourth place.

The U.S. Open was taking its toll on others, particularly slowing the progress of Mediate, who drifted back at just the right time. He tripped at the 15th when he couldn't get to the green after an errant drive. His third from the rough he couldn't control and the ball bounded over the green into a bunker. He blasted out and two-putted for double-bogey 6 to fall to one under par for the championship.

"I made one little mistake and got ripped, but that's what the Open does to you," Mediate said.

That slip-up put Westwood in charge, and he had been steady, not just all day Saturday, but all throughout the week—perhaps the most solid and steady of any of the competitors. In 54 holes he had suffered nothing higher than a bogey, and he had only chalked up six of those. However, he also had a mere eight birdies, and his putting stroke was letting him down on several good birdie looks. He had another at the par-5 18th, but his entreaty went unanswered from a mere 6 feet.

But it looked like that lead would hold, especially when Woods came up short and left, near a bunker, in thick kikuyugrass at the par-4 17th. The lie wasn't particularly good, but it was on an upslope, and Woods chopped down on it, squirting the ball up fast but also too far. It landed not more than a foot in front of the hole, then hit the flagstick and fell in.

"That has no business going in the hole," said Woods, who reacted sheepishly to the result of the hit-and-hope stroke. He pulled off his hat with his right hand, hung his head in embarrassment and laughed as he peeked over at his caddie, Steve Williams. He admitted later that the thought running through his head was one of wonder: "You've got to be kidding me."

"I was thinking, 'Don't make a 6.' And I made a 3."

And there was one more 3 to go. Woods finally found the fairway, just his sixth of the day, at the 18th with an intentional slice. That left him 227 yards from the hole location tucked behind the only water hazard on the course. His 5-wood was well struck, landing safely over the water and about 40 feet behind the hole. Again, he knew what the putt would do, and he merely allowed for more break in the left-to-right putt given the swiftness of the green. There was never a doubt about its destination.

Seated in the interview room about 600 yards away from that latest salvo from Woods, Westwood, winner of 29 tournament titles, was taking in a few questions about his resurgence after falling from No. 4 in the world rankings down to around No. 200 in 2002. He couldn't see the large television off his left shoulder showing Woods knock him down one disappointing peg on the leaderboard with that improbable, impeccable eagle.

So, the next question just seconds after Woods' eagle, went like this:

"Sorry, but you're not the clubhouse leader any more, but you are one of the few people in the world who does have the experience of coming back and beating Tiger Woods on a Sunday. It was a long time ago, but does that mean anything to you going into tomorrow?"

On the 17th hole, Woods couldn't believe his luck.

Mike Weir (216) shot 69, climbing to tie for 11th.

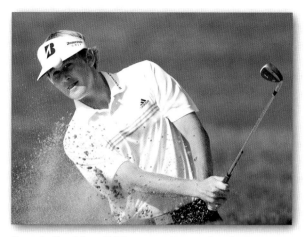

Brandt Snedeker (217) was under par for the first time.

"It's better to have done it than not done it," he replied with a grin.

That occurred in 2000 at the Deutsche Bank SAP Open, in Hamburg, Germany, when he was playing a similarly splendid brand of golf. Westwood fired a final-round 8-under 64 to overtake Woods for one of his six titles that year.

Westwood, whose best previous Open was a tie for fifth in 2000 when he finished a mere 17 strokes behind Woods at Pebble Beach, certainly fit the profile of a contender at this Open. He didn't have many, having withdrawn from the BMW European PGA Championship after contracting tonsillitis, and his only start since then had been The Players, where he missed the cut. "I didn't hit too many balls coming into this week. I had a couple of weeks off, which I don't usually do in a major championship, one week off, but not two. I kept my expectations low, and it's sometimes easy to go out when you don't have any expectations."

Low expectations were the common denominator among the pursuers when the sun went down on the Pacific Coast.

"It's going to take a ridiculous round by one of us to beat him," Mediate estimated. "If we go out and shoot four or five under par, one of us, you never know. But you can't ever count on anything. It's just you can't really predict anything that's going to happen. When he has a lead, he's never lost. So that means he's never lost. So chances are that could happen tomorrow. It's not over yet. And

John Merrick (216) was a surprising contender.

On the 18th hole, Woods was successful from 40 feet for his second eagle in five holes.

I'm sure he'll tell you the same thing. Because this is a U.S. Open course, and you just don't know what the heck is going to happen sometimes.

"But it's going to take something crazy."

Which was more or less what Woods perpetrated in the third round. Crazy stuff. Wonderful, crazy stuff.

"Mr. Woods, Mr. Woods, Mr. Woods, are you insane? Are you out of your mind?" Mediate shouted, drawing laughs, after he snuck in among a group of reporters talking to Woods just outside the scoring room.

No, he wasn't insane. But you had to wonder just how much he was driving everyone else to that special place that England's Paul Casey said the U.S. Open can send so many players—a padded cell.

Hunter Mahan (215) had risen to the top 10.

Rocco Mediate (283) gave it his all. 'I have nothing left right now. I'm toast,' Mediate said after his 71.

108th U.S. OPEN
Fourth Round

The last thing he wanted, with an injured leg hurting worse by the day, was to have to keep playing. But it was also the one thing he wanted more than anything else.

Tiger Woods already had filled up the week with transcendent moments and trance-inducing shots, but late on Sunday afternoon, as the sun drifted over the mesa and toward the Pacific Ocean, Woods needed one more piece of magic. Play in the 108th U.S. Open Championship had all but expired, and Woods stood alone—at least as best he could—against the forces of expectations and mounting odds and the suffocating pressure of the final hole of a major championship.

Undoubtedly, he wouldn't have wanted to be anywhere else.

A gritty but untidy final round at Torrey Pines Golf Course had brought him to this place—a predicament, really—where he had to make a birdie at the par-5 home hole, the 72nd hole of the championship, to tie Rocco Mediate and send the championship into a playoff. A 12-foot putt was the challenge. Twelve feet, and he would stay alive. Twelve feet, and a 14th major championship was still in play. Twelve feet, and the legend would grow, if that were possible.

"The putt was probably about two and a half balls outside right. And the green wasn't very smooth," Woods explained in setting the scene. "I kept telling myself, make a pure stroke; if it bounces in or out, so be it, at least I can hold my head up high and hit a pure stroke.

"I hit it exactly where I wanted it, and it went in."

Of course it did. It bounced along on the frumpy, bumpy Poa *annua* grass, somehow gained just enough traction on the intended line, caught the edge of the hole, and swirled to the back corner and then down. It was a few seconds of mastery that deserved not one fist pump but the stereo version, and Woods let loose with both arms working like pistons.

The U.S. Open was headed to an 18-hole playoff.

"Unbelievable," said Mediate with a shake of his head as he watched on a television monitor in the scoring room, some 200 yards from Torrey South's 18th green. "I knew he'd make it. That's what he does."

Perhaps everyone knew. But no one could have known that it would be Mediate, the friendly but fragile veteran from Pennsylvania, who would be the man pushing the No. 1 player to the brink of defeat. If Woods were going to see his perfect streak of protecting 54-hole leads in major championships end, the favorite to deal the disappointing blow was Tiger's final-round playing partner, Lee Westwood, who had been uncannily solid and steady all week.

Instead, Mediate, who had to survive a playoff in sectional qualifying just to get in the main event, was the last hurdle for Woods. Mediate fired an even-par 71 on Torrey South and sauntered into the house with a 1-under 283 total to become the first player since 2004 at Shinnecock Hills Golf Club to break par in the U.S. Open. Woods, with a 2-over 73 for his 283 aggregate, became the second.

"I bet you're surprised to see me here again," Mediate, age 45, said to the media with a huge grin.

Tiger Woods (283) was wincing after his second tee shot.

Yes, and the only thing more surprising was how it all unfolded to set up the amazing final sequence of events.

Playing in the final group for the sixth time in the last eight majors, Woods had admitted in a brief television interview Saturday night that his knee wasn't getting any better. There were whispers that he might "go the way of Big Brown" at the Open—unable to finish on Sunday the way the large and powerful Triple Crown hopeful couldn't at the recent Belmont Stakes. But there was no way Woods was going to miss it, not after all he already had been through.

A crowd of almost 60,000 wasn't going to miss this day either. When Woods and Westwood arrived on the tee for their 1:30 p.m. PDT starting time, fans stood 25 rows deep behind the tee and almost as deep down the length of the hole, while those in the top rows of the bleachers on the adjacent 18th hole turned around to watch the beginning of what was shaping up to be an epic round.

The weekend included both Father's Day and Flag Day, and the latter was noted by sailors off the third green.

Fourth Round

Rocco Mediate	69 - 71 - 72 - 71 – 283	-1	
Tiger Woods	72 - 68 - 70 - 73 – 283	-1	
Lee Westwood	70 - 71 - 70 - 73 – 284	E	
Robert Karlsson	70 - 70 - 75 - 71 – 286	+2	
D.J. Trahan	72 - 69 - 73 - 72 – 286	+2	
Carl Pettersson	71 - 71 - 77 - 68 – 287	+3	
John Merrick	73 - 72 - 71 - 71 – 287	+3	
Miguel Angel Jimenez	75 - 66 - 74 - 72 – 287	+3	
Heath Slocum	75 - 74 - 74 - 65 – 288	+4	
Eric Axley	69 - 79 - 71 - 69 – 288	+4	
Brandt Snedeker	76 - 73 - 68 - 71 – 288	+4	
Camilo Villegas	73 - 71 - 71 - 73 – 288	+4	
Geoff Ogilvy	69 - 73 - 72 - 74 – 288	+4	

Mediate was among the leaders of greens hit.

It would become mostly an odyssey, starting with the confounding first hole. Woods snaphooked his tee shot over the heads of the gallery on the left to begin a hacker's tour of the 448-yard par 4. Out of a poor lie, Woods pulled his second shot left a bit and hit a tree. His third clipped a branch and failed to reach the fairway. The fourth shot he could only hack out short of the green. A deftly played pitch left him 3 feet that he was able to negotiate for a double-bogey 6. That put him seven over par for the week on his opening hole, and when he followed with his fourth three-putt of the week at the short par-4 second hole, Woods was all the way back to even par—and trailing.

Westwood, who bogeyed the first hole with his own adventures in the opposite rough, was the new leader, and though his putter still wasn't fully cooperating, the Englishman was avoiding additional blunders. When he matched Woods' birdie at the par-5 ninth with a 4 of his own from 5 feet, Westwood remained one in front of Woods and Mediate and two in front of 2006 Open champion Geoff Ogilvy.

All three were tied 10 minutes later when Westwood bogeyed after sculling his second shot over the green from a fairway bunker. Meanwhile, Ogilvy and two-time champion Ernie Els had been hanging around, but Ogilvy encountered putting problems and fell back, while Els would come

After a penalty drop at the 13th, Woods took bogey, his first at that par-5 hole in 36 official rounds.

Eric Axley (288) shot 69 to finish in the top 10.

unglued with a sloppy par at the drivable 14th hole and a triple bogey at the 15th.

When Woods birdied the 11th with a 3-foot putt and Westwood bogeyed the 10th and 12th, it appeared that normalcy was returning to the proceedings. No such thing this week. Mediate got up and down from the right greenside bunker at the 14th, set up at just 267 yards, for a birdie to climb to two under par just as Woods and Westwood were both making bogeys at the par-5 13th, a

HOLE 14 SCORECARD

How the par-4 14th hole played the first three rounds at 435 yards and in the fourth round at 267 yards:

First Three Rounds at 435 Yards

Players	Eagles	Birdies	Average	Rank
390	0	32	4.344	5

Fourth Round at 267 Yards

Players	Eagles	Birdies	Average	Rank
80	1	26	3.812	17

A birdie opportunity at the 17th slipped past as Mediate missed a chance to go two strokes ahead.

hole Woods had already eagled twice and had never bogeyed in the 35 official rounds he had previously played on the South Course. Both men pulled their second shots left in the canyon and had to take penalty drops. It was a risk Woods didn't need to take, and it cost him.

Westwood birdied the 14th after driving the green to end a string of three bogeys in four holes (after making five bogeys in the first three rounds) to get back to even par, but Woods, after laying up, had to settle for par 4. He was running out of holes.

"It looked like I was shooting myself out of the tournament," Woods admitted.

But Mediate couldn't get home cleanly. He pulled his drive at the par-4 15th in the deep rough, leading to a bogey that dropped him back to one under par. An opening for Woods? Only until he also missed the fairway at the 15th and then came up well short in the rough for his second shot. He missed a putt from 12 feet, took bogey and slid back to even par, tied with Westwood.

All week golfers, fans, experts and USGA

Robert Karlsson (286) shot 71 to tie for fourth.

Stewart Cink (289) improved 10 shots to 67.

Michael Thompson (292) was the low amateur.

officials figured that the 18th hole, set up Sunday at 527 yards and reachable for much of the field, would swing the championship. With a one-stroke lead, Mediate could get the pendulum to tilt in his direction if he could somehow make a birdie and put two strokes between himself and the two in the final group.

Mediate, ranked 158th in the world and who two years ago was in bad shape physically with his ailing back and had taken up a side job as an on-course reporter for Golf Channel, gave himself an opportunity for the killing blow. He drove in the fairway and laid up to 106 yards for his third shot. But he struck it a bit too firmly and watched it settle 30 feet above the hole. His first putt, which trundled left to right, never looked at the hole. He tapped in for par. There was nothing more he could do but sign his card and watch the finish like everyone else.

"I did the absolute best that I could. I have nothing left right now. I'm toast," said Mediate, who made only one bogey over the final 12 holes.

Back on the tee, things weren't going well for the final two. Westwood pulled his tee shot into the left fairway bunker; Woods pushed his into the right bunker. Both laid up, but Woods got sloppy on a 9-iron out of a perfect lie and ballooned his second shot into the right rough. He spun around and swung his club in anger and frustration.

"I had just an absolute pure lie," Woods conceded. "If I was in a practice round, I would have

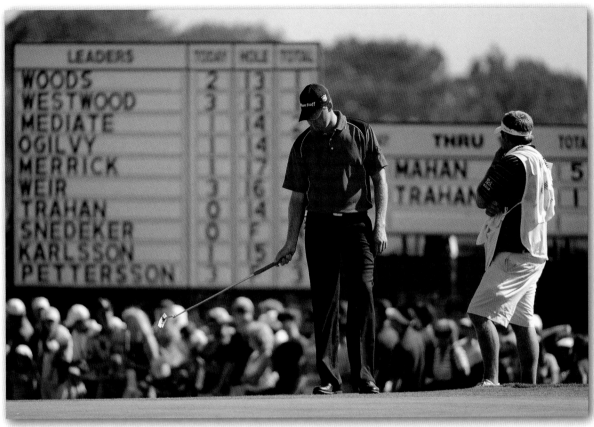

D.J. Trahan (286) took bogeys at two of the last three holes, and shot 72 for a share of fourth place.

gone for it. I stuck a 9-iron in the sand and hit it straight right. I was trying to play off the right side, but not that far right."

Like Mediate, Westwood got too bold on his approach shot and powered it 25 feet past the flagstick. And like Mediate, he didn't read enough break or speed on the green and had to settle for par and a round of 73 and 284 total, one stroke too many.

"It's sickening not to be in the playoff tomorrow," Westwood said. "But all in all, I played pretty good all week. And if somebody said, 'You're going to have a chance for a playoff on Monday,' then I would have probably taken that at the start of the week. I think I've proved to myself and a few others that I think there is a major championship in me."

Now there was only Woods. He and his caddie, Steve Williams, mulled over club choice. The yardage, 95 to the front edge of the green and 101 yards to the hole, was right for his 56-degree wedge, but

Carl Pettersson (287) had 68 to tie for sixth.

61

John Merrick (287) closed with two 71s.

Retief Goosen (289) finished well with 67.

he decided to plow through the thick kikuyu, bad knee and all, with his 60-degree wedge. "It came out perfect," Woods said.

It had to.

Then came the putt, which he fretted could "plinko out," thus adding another word to the golfing lexicon. He soon added to the amazing history of the U.S. Open. His golf ball looked like it would stay on the edge of the hole, but it leaned left with perhaps a foot to go. Woods started to backpedal as the putt neared the hole, paused and seemed to hold his breath as it caught the lip, and then clenched and pumped both fists and let out a scream of joy and relief after it dropped.

It was a moment reminiscent of the 9-foot birdie putt Woods had to convert at the 72nd hole at the 2000 PGA Championship at Valhalla Golf Club near Louisville, Ky. Woods went on to defeat Bob May in a three-hole playoff for the third leg of what became known as the Tiger Slam, when he won four major championships in a row, culminating in the 2001 Masters.

"It feels very similar to what Valhalla felt like," Woods said. "If I didn't make that putt, I don't get to continue to keep playing. At best, I gave myself a chance to win the tournament tomorrow. And that's all I can ask for."

The U.S. Open had its first playoff since 2001, when Retief Goosen dispatched Mark Brooks at Southern Hills Country Club in Tulsa, Okla.

While Westwood finished one painful stroke out of the playoff, Robert Karlsson of Sweden and American D.J. Trahan were pleased with their highest career finishes in major championships after tying for fourth place. Karlsson closed with an even-par 71 and Trahan a 72, both in coming home at 286.

Spain's Miguel Angel Jimenez, Sweden's Carl Pettersson and American John Merrick tied for sixth at 287. Pettersson had a round of 68. Then came five tied for ninth at 288 including a former champion, Ogilvy, from Australia, who finished with 74. The others at 288 were Colombia's Camilo Villegas and Americans Brandt Snedeker, Heath Slocum and Eric Axley. Slocum jumped from a tie for 58th into his first top-10 finish in a major

A large gallery along the 18th hole awaited the final groups.

after firing the low round of the championship, a 6-under 65. Axley finished as he had started, with 69.

Former U.S. Open champions Els and Retief Goosen, both from South Africa, tied for 14th at 289 along with another Australian, Rod Pampling, and Stewart Cink, an American. Cink and Goosen both finished with 67s.

Phil Mickelson enjoyed his best round of the championship, a 3-under 68 that tied him for 18th at 290 with seven others, including Sergio Garcia and Mike Weir.

Michael Thompson, the runner-up in the 2007 U.S. Amateur Championship, shot a final-round 72, his best score of the week, and claimed the honor as low amateur, tied for 29th at 292.

There was still golf to be played, however, to determine who would be the best for the week. The odds were all stacked in Woods' favor, given his 13 major titles and 18-3 record in playoffs, including

Heath Slocum (288) shot 65, low round of the week.

Both arms were pumping after Woods holed from 12 feet to secure his place in the Monday playoff.

10-1 on the PGA Tour. Two of those wins were in majors, at the aforementioned 2000 PGA and at the 2005 Masters, where he beat Chris DiMarco at the first extra hole.

Mediate's five career PGA Tour titles included two victories in overtime. He also got the better of Woods in the 1999 Phoenix Open (now the FBR Open) in Scottsdale, Ariz., in his only other close encounter with the world's top-ranked player.

"I'm playing against a monster tomorrow morning," Mediate said with noted relish in his voice. "I've got to get excited to play. I get to play against the best player that ever played. I want to see what I have against the man. Whatever happens, happens. I'm happy that I'm here and I will give it everything I have and see what we do.

"I don't know how you make odds on that," he added. "But I have nothing to lose, I really don't. I can't believe I'm in this situation. I can't wait to go see what I've got against the man. I can't wait to see what I've got against him. I know what he has."

He was referring to Woods' game. Probably his desire and powers of concentration, too. But only Woods knew what he had left health-wise.

"I don't have much of a choice. It's going to have to hold up. It is what it is," Woods said when asked if he could go 18 more holes. "I'm looking forward to it. I've never been in this position before in a U.S. Open. I still have a chance going into tomorrow."

Which is all he ever wants, just a chance.

Lee Westwood (284) had a playoff chance at the 18th.

People soon knew what Tiger Woods meant when he said: 'This is probably the greatest tournament I ever had.'

When the 108th U.S. Open Championship was finally over, when he had vanquished the last opponent after 91 holes that were as exciting to watch as they were excruciating for him to play, Tiger Woods, the U.S. Open trophy in hand for the third time, summed up his week with a startling piece of personal reflection.

"This is probably the greatest tournament I've ever had," he said.

Given his body of work since he turned professional in 1996—or even before that with an unprecedented six straight U.S. Junior Amateur and Amateur titles—the admission, on its face, considering the known facts at the time, possessed a distinct whiff of hyperbole.

After all, Woods had submitted some mind-boggling performances in major championships, starting with his first as a professional at the 1997 Masters. He won the first of his four Masters by a record 12 strokes with an 18-under-par 270 score, also a record.

He won his first U.S. Open in 2000 at Pebble Beach Golf Links by 15 strokes with a record-tying 272 total and broke the major championship record for winning margin that Old Tom Morris set in 1862.

He won his first British Open, also in 2000, at the Old Course at St. Andrews by eight strokes with another scoring mark of 19-under 269, and in the process became the youngest player to secure the career Grand Slam. So impeccable was his performance that he never strayed into a single bunker all week.

He capped off his amazing 2000 major run with an 18-under 270 performance at the PGA Championship at Valhalla Golf Club in Louisville, Ky., but had to go three extra holes before dispatching Bob May for his third major win of the year. In so doing, he became the first player since Ben Hogan to accomplish the feat. Of course, with his 2001 Masters victory, he became the first player to hold all four professional major trophies at the same time.

Still, none of it compared to his sudden-death playoff victory over upstart Rocco Mediate, achieved after a scheduled 18-hole showdown ended in a tie with both men carding 71s, level par on Torrey Pines South.

Woods provided context to his astonishing assessment two days later, and he put the entire week in a perspective that induced a higher degree of incredulity. On June 17, the No. 1 player in the world and newly minted U.S. Open champion announced that his 2008 season was coming to an end because his knee required reconstructive surgery.

It turns out that Woods had competed in the U.S. Open on a left leg that he had no business putting through the rigors of a golf championship. Not only was Woods suffering from a torn anterior cruciate ligament in his left knee—which he injured nearly a year ago while on a training run after the British Open—but also he had to contend with stress fractures in his left tibia, which were the result of a rehabilitation regimen that proved to be too ambitious following the arthroscopic surgery he had after the Masters.

He underwent the follow-up procedure, the fourth operation on his knee, on June 24. No timetable was given for his return.

Woods was up by three strokes after 10 holes.

There isn't likely to be an expiration date on the historic momentousness of what Woods did. He may not have been Hogan, winning the 1950 U.S. Open after his near-fatal automobile collision with a Greyhound bus, but Woods exhibited an ineffable sense of determination that was sure to be talked about for years to come.

"In light of the revelation about Tiger's health, it makes his performance in the U.S. Open that much more phenomenal," said four-time winner Jack Nicklaus, who saw Woods climb within four of his record of 18 professional major titles. "I have always said that the U.S. Open is the most difficult and complete examination of a golfer, and for him to persevere with a damaged knee and stress fractures is a testament not only to his ability, but also his tremendously high level of competitiveness. He was obviously in pain, but he played right through it. To have a will as strong as that, I take my hat off to him."

Like every previous round Woods played in this Open championship, the playoff featured interludes of vintage golf and periods of fallibil-

After hitting his tee shot at the 15th into a bunker, Woods took par 4 while Rocco Mediate birdied to lead by one.

ity. While he had mostly knocked off the rust from his two months of inactivity, Woods couldn't quite shake the discomfort. His only amelioration came from the satisfaction of hitting just enough great shots in between the unforced errors.

"I just kept going forward," said Woods, who hadn't walked 18 holes since the final round of the Masters. "I dealt with a few things this week and just had to keep plugging along, wasn't feeling my best. I just had to keep battling back."

In a rerun of the previous day, Woods extricated himself from a desperate situation of his own making at the 18th hole after he had seemingly taken control of the championship.

With a crowd of about 25,000 in tow, Woods, age 32, and Mediate, trying to become the oldest U.S. Open champion at 45 years, 6 months, matched wits, shots and pained expressions. Woods appeared to seize firm control when he birdied the sixth and seventh to erase an early bogey and get to one under par, while Mediate, looking uneasy, bogeyed the fifth after a poor bunker shot, three-putted the par-5 ninth from 18 feet for a bogey and took 5 for another bogey at the 10th hole.

The margin was three shots. Mediate appeared spent.

But then Woods, uncharacteristically, provided an opening. He bogeyed the 11th after driving in a bunker. Then he bogeyed No. 12 the same way. Seeing the thin layer of hope, Mediate rattled off three straight birdies, only one of which Woods could match.

"I threw everything I had, the kitchen sink, everything right at him," said Mediate, who had never before come so close to winning a major title. "I was three down through 10. It could have been over pretty quick, and he hit that ball in the bunker. Not that I felt he was going to bogey, but it's not the easiest shot, and I hit a good shot and all of a sudden bang, bang, bang, I pick up three, four shots, and in a few holes, and I'm one up."

It was just that fast. Mediate converted a 5-footer at the par-5 13th to match Woods' birdie and then got up and down for a second birdie after driving to the front edge of the green at the 14th, which again had been shortened to 267 yards. At

With three holes to play, Mediate thought he would win.

the 15th, a curling 20-foot putt went down for his third birdie in a row, and it took Woods down one more notch.

"I thought I was going to win after that putt went in on 15," Mediate said. "I said, 'If I can keep hitting good shot after good shot, which I pretty much did, I'm going to win this golf tournament.'"

But he still had to navigate the par-5 18th, and once again, after they matched pars at the 16th and 17th, Mediate's failure to make a birdie and put away Woods at the home hole ultimately proved to be his downfall. While he played smartly in laying up to leave himself a 20-footer for birdie and the victory, Woods belted a drive and a towering 4-iron from 217 yards safely over the pond for a 45-foot eagle chance.

Mediate had the championship on his putter after Woods left that attempt about 4 feet from the hole. "I said to myself, 'You've waited your whole life for this putt, just don't lag it,'" Mediate said.

He didn't, but he didn't have the line and ran it 3 feet past, forcing him to shake that in to force

With his third shot on the sudden-death hole, Mediate chipped 18 feet past the hole, and Woods won with his par.

sudden death after Woods firmly sank the straight-in tying putt.

With all that the two men had been through, a lengthy showdown seemed inevitable and fitting. But Mediate, perhaps a bit fatigued, pull-hooked his drive into the left fairway bunker at the par-4 seventh hole and found his ball in an awkward lie. He missed the green with his second shot from 184 yards, watching the ball careen off a cart path and up against the bleachers. After a chip to 18 feet past the hole, the veteran missed the par putt.

After providing so many knee-buckling and dramatic moments, Woods had a chance to perform routinely, and his par ended the championship.

"Great fight," Woods told Mediate as they embraced on the seventh green.

"Obviously, I would have loved to win," Mediate said. "I don't know what else to say. They wanted a show. They got one.

"I never quit. I never quit," he added. "I've been beaten down a few times and came back, and I got what I wanted. I got a chance to beat the best player in the world. And I came up just a touch short. Nothing he does amazes me."

While Mediate, the heavy underdog, wondered how he had come so close only to lose the biggest prize of his career, Woods was no less confounded by an outcome that eventually ended in his favor.

"All things considered, I don't know how I ended up in this position, to be honest with you," Woods said. "It was a long week. There was a lot of doubt, a lot of questions going into the week. And here we are 91 holes later.

"I'm glad I'm done," Woods added. "I really don't feel like playing anymore. It's sore."

It must have been quite sore for him to talk about not wanting to play. But, surely, he knew he had done enough. He knew at the time, when few others did, that he had accomplished something extraordinary.

'Great fight,' Woods told Mediate afterward, and Rocco said to the media: 'They wanted a show. They got one.'

His swing coach, Hank Haney, was among the handful of people who understood the extent of the injury Woods was fighting to overcome. "This is the greatest thing he's ever done in golf," Haney said. "He's done this before—laying off—but he didn't do it without preparing. That's what made me apprehensive. That's why this is the greatest win he's ever had. It may be the greatest thing anyone's ever done in golf."

The grit and courage Woods displayed drew comparisons to Hogan, but Woods would have none of that.

"Well, I was not in as bad of shape as Ben was," Woods pointed out. "Geez, he was in the hospital and he didn't know if he was ever going to walk again. I knew I could walk, it's just going to be a little bit on the slow side. But I was just trying to get through this week. Everyone plays with knick-knack injuries, and here, there, whatever it is, and Roc's done it pretty much his entire career with his bad back. Guys have that, you have injuries, and you play through it and suck it up and get it done."

Woods, who improved to 44-3 when holding at least a share of the 54-hole lead, got it done, all right. In his 500th week atop the Official World Golf Ranking, Woods won his ninth USGA title, tying him with the great Bob Jones for most all time. He won the career Grand Slam a third time over, tying Nicklaus for that distinction. He won his 65th PGA Tour title, breaking a tie with Hogan and moving into third place alone behind Nicklaus (73) and Sam Snead (82). He won for the seventh time as a professional on the same golf course, another record. He tied Hale Irwin for the second-most Open titles, one behind the record four titles won by Willie Anderson, Jones, Hogan and Nicklaus.

In the end, most importantly, Woods had shown how much the spirit of the game is alive in him.

108th
U.S. OPEN
Torrey Pines
Golf Course

June 12-16, 2008, Torrey Pines South Golf Course, San Diego, Calif.

Rd. 1	Rd. 2	Rd. 3	Rd. 4	Contestant	Rounds				Total	Prize
T19	T2	1	1	Tiger Woods	72	68	70	73	283	$1,350,000.00
T3	T2	3	2	Rocco Mediate	69	71	72	71	283	810,000.00
(Woods defeated Mediate 5-4 on 19th playoff hole, following 18-hole playoff scores of 71-71)										
T7	T5	T2	3	Lee Westwood	70	71	70	73	284	491,995.00
T7	T2	T6	T4	Robert Karlsson	70	70	75	71	286	307,303.00
T19	T5	T4	T4	D.J. Trahan	72	69	73	72	286	307,303.00
T12	T9	T24	T6	Carl Pettersson	71	71	77	68	287	220,686.00
T31	T22	T11	T6	John Merrick	73	72	71	71	287	220,686.00
T64	T5	T6	T6	Miguel Angel Jimenez	75	66	74	72	287	220,686.00
T64	T65	T58	T9	Heath Slocum	75	74	74	65	288	160,769.00
T3	T49	T24	T9	Eric Axley	69	79	71	69	288	160,769.00
T85	T65	T15	T9	Brandt Snedeker	76	73	68	71	288	160,769.00
T31	T16	T6	T9	Camilo Villegas	73	71	71	73	288	160,769.00
T3	T9	T4	T9	Geoff Ogilvy	69	73	72	74	288	160,769.00
T19	T22	T47	T14	Stewart Cink	72	73	77	67	289	122,159.00
T85	T22	T47	T14	Retief Goosen	76	69	77	67	289	122,159.00
T49	T16	T24	T14	Rod Pampling	74	70	75	70	289	122,159.00
T7	T9	T11	T14	Ernie Els	70	72	74	73	289	122,159.00
T12	T35	T47	T18	Phil Mickelson	71	75	76	68	290	87,230.00
T100	T65	T35	T18	Chad Campbell	77	72	71	70	290	87,230.00
T49	T65	T24	T18	Ryuji Imada	74	75	70	71	290	87,230.00
T31	T49	T15	T18	Brandt Jobe	73	75	69	73	290	87,230.00
T85	T35	T11	T18	Sergio Garcia	76	70	70	74	290	87,230.00
T31	T42	T11	T18	Mike Weir	73	74	69	74	290	87,230.00
T7	T9	T6	T18	Robert Allenby	70	72	73	75	290	87,230.00
T19	T35	T6	T18	Hunter Mahan	72	74	69	75	290	87,230.00
T31	T35	T42	T26	Adam Scott	73	73	75	70	291	61,252.00
T31	T65	T24	T26	Boo Weekley	73	76	70	72	291	61,252.00
T49	T65	T24	T26	Anthony Kim	74	75	70	72	291	61,252.00
T64	T22	T58	T29	Bart Bryant	75	70	78	69	292	48,482.00
T49	T42	T35	T29	*Michael Thompson	74	73	73	72	292	Medal
T31	T65	T35	T29	Steve Stricker	73	76	71	72	292	48,482.00
T12	T22	T24	T29	Patrick Sheehan	71	74	74	73	292	48,482.00
T126	T65	T24	T29	Jeff Quinney	79	70	70	73	292	48,482.00
T19	T16	T19	T29	Scott Verplank	72	72	74	74	292	48,482.00
T49	T42	T19	T29	Aaron Baddeley	74	73	71	74	292	48,482.00
T64	T49	T58	T36	Pat Perez	75	73	75	70	293	35,709.00
T31	T49	T58	T36	Daniel Chopra	73	75	75	70	293	35,709.00
T112	T22	T47	T36	Padraig Harrington	78	67	77	71	293	35,709.00
T19	T42	T47	T36	Jon Mills	72	75	75	71	293	35,709.00
T64	T42	T47	T36	Justin Leonard	75	72	75	71	293	35,709.00
T12	T16	T42	T36	Andres Romero	71	73	77	72	293	35,709.00
T49	T49	T42	T36	Todd Hamilton	74	74	73	72	293	35,709.00
T12	T42	T35	T36	Joe Ogilvie	71	76	73	73	293	35,709.00
T31	T16	T24	T36	Robert Dinwiddie	73	71	75	74	293	35,709.00
T3	1	T19	T36	Stuart Appleby	69	70	79	75	293	35,709.00
T49	T22	T19	T36	Jim Furyk	74	71	73	75	293	35,709.00
T19	T14	T15	T36	Oliver Wilson	72	71	74	76	293	35,709.00

Rd. 1	Rd. 2	Rd. 3	Rd. 4	Contestant	Rounds				Total	Prize
T64	T65	T58	T48	Jarrod Lyle	75	74	74	71	294	23,985.00
T64	T14	T47	T48	John Rollins	75	68	79	72	294	23,985.00
T31	T35	T47	T48	Matt Kuchar	73	73	76	72	294	23,985.00
T49	T35	T42	T48	Dustin Johnson	74	72	75	73	294	23,985.00
T31	T22	T24	T48	Tim Clark	73	72	74	75	294	23,985.00
T64	T42	T66	T53	Ben Crane	75	72	77	71	295	20,251.00
T112	T49	T66	T53	Soren Hansen	78	70	76	71	295	20,251.00
T1	T22	T58	T53	Kevin Streelman	68	77	78	72	295	20,251.00
T64	T22	T19	T53	Martin Kaymer	75	77	71	72	295	20,251.00
T19	T15	T15	T53	Davis Love III	72	69	76	78	295	20,251.00
T49	T49	T70	T58	Stephen Ames	74	74	77	71	296	18,664.00
T31	T22	T35	T58	Rory Sabbatini	73	72	75	76	296	18,664.00
T31	T49	T70	T60	Nick Watney	73	75	77	72	297	17,691.00
T7	T65	T70	T60	*Rickie Fowler	70	79	76	72	297	
T85	T65	T58	T60	Alastair Forsyth	76	73	74	74	297	17,691.00
T31	T22	T47	T60	Brett Quigley	73	72	77	75	297	17,691.00
T85	T49	T35	T60	David Toms	76	72	72	77	297	17,691.00
T31	T49	T75	T65	John Mallinger	73	75	78	72	298	16,514.00
T12	T65	T70	T65	Vijay Singh	71	78	76	73	298	16,514.00
T126	T65	T70	T65	Paul Casey	79	70	76	73	298	16,514.00
T64	T49	T35	T65	Trevor Immelman	75	73	72	78	298	16,514.00
T31	T35	T66	T69	*Derek Fathauer	73	73	78	75	299	
T49	T22	T47	T69	D.A. Points	74	71	77	77	299	15,778.00
T85	T65	T79	T71	Andrew Dresser	76	73	79	72	300	15,189.00
T100	T49	T47	T71	Andrew Svoboda	77	71	74	78	300	15,189.00
T19	T16	T42	T71	Woody Austin	72	72	77	79	300	15,189.00
T100	T65	T75	T74	Jesper Parnevik	77	72	77	75	301	14,306.00
T19	T49	T66	T74	Ian Leggatt	72	76	76	77	301	14,306.00
T1	T49	T58	T74	Justin Hicks	68	80	75	78	301	14,306.00
T85	T49	T75	77	Ross McGowan	76	72	78	77	303	13,718.00
T49	T49	T79	T78	Rich Beem	74	74	80	76	304	13,276.00
T64	T65	78	T78	Chris Kirk	75	74	78	77	304	13,276.00
T12	T9	T24		Luke Donald	71	71	77		WD	2,000.00

Jon Turcott	77	73	150	Michael Allen	78	75	153	*Jordan Cox	80	77	157
Scott Sterling	80	70	150	Charles Howell III	75	78	153	Sean English	75	82	157
Zach Johnson	76	74	150	*Kevin Tway	75	78	153	Phil Archer	78	81	159
Toru Taniguchi	74	76	150	Jason Bohn	76	77	153	Jay Choi	79	80	159
J.B. Holmes	75	75	150	Fredrik Jacobson	74	79	153	*Jeff Wilson	78	81	159
Robert Garrigus	77	73	150	Lee Janzen	75	78	153	Steve Flesch	78	81	159
*Kyle Stanley	72	78	150	Shingo Katayama	77	76	153	Jeffrey Bors	81	79	160
Casey Wittenberg	72	78	150	D.J. Brigman	79	75	154	Chris Stroud	84	77	161
Hunter Haas	80	70	150	Henrik Stenson	78	76	154	Philippe Gasnier	86	75	161
Thomas Levet	74	76	150	Bubba Watson	77	77	154	Michael Campbell	78	83	161
Mathew Goggin	77	73	150	Charlie Beljan	76	79	155	Yohann Benson	83	78	161
Rob Rashell	81	70	151	Angel Cabrera	79	76	155	Artemio Murakami	79	83	162
Richard Sterne	76	75	151	Nick Dougherty	78	77	155	Bobby Collins	84	78	162
Ben Curtis	75	76	151	Jason Gore	79	76	155	Garrett Chaussard	80	82	162
Justin Rose	79	72	151	Dean Wilson	76	79	155	Brian Kortan	78	84	162
Mark O'Meara	75	76	151	Joey Lamielle	76	79	155	*Jimmy Henderson	81	82	163
Ross Fisher	73	78	151	Travis Bertoni	82	73	155	Fernando Figueroa	78	85	163
Steve Marino	73	78	151	Colin Montgomerie	79	77	156	Niclas Fasth	78	86	164
John Ellis	77	74	151	Kevin Silva	80	76	156	*Gary Wolstenholme	83	82	165
Peter Tomasulo	76	75	151	Bob Gaus	80	76	156	*Michael Quagliano	86	81	167
David Hearn	76	75	151	Craig Barlow	80	76	156	Mike Gilmore	86	81	167
Scott Piercy	78	73	151	Brad Bryant	77	79	156	Chris Devlin	84	83	167
K.J. Choi	74	77	151	Craig Parry	75	81	156	Brian Bergstol	86	81	167
*Nick Taylor	77	75	152	Johan Edfors	79	77	156	Ian Poulter	78		WD
Jonathan Byrd	75	77	152	Jerry Kelly	75	82	157	Mark Calcavecchia			WD
Michael Letzig	77	75	152								

Professionals not returning 72-hole scores received $2,000 each.

*Denotes amateur

108th U.S. OPEN Statistics

Hole	1	2	3	4	5	6	7	8	9	10	11	12	13	14	15	16	17	18	Total	
Par	**4**	**4**	**3**	**4**	**4**	**4**	**4**	**3**	**5**	**4**	**3**	**4**	**5**	**4**	**4**	**3**	**4**	**5**	**71**	
Tiger Woods																				
Round 1	[6]	4	3	(3)	4	4	4	(2)	(4)	4	3	4	5	[6]	4	3	4	5	72	
Round 2 (started on hole 10)	(3)	(3)	3	(3)	(3)	4	4	3	(4)	[5]	3	[5]	(3)	4	4	[4]	[5]	5	68	
Round 3	[6]	4	3	[5]	4	4	(3)	3	5	4	3	[5]	(3)	[5]	4	3	(3)	(3)	70	
Round 4	[6]	[5]	3	4	4	4	4	3	(4)	4	(2)	4	[6]	4	[5]	3	4	(4)	73	283
Playoff	4	4	[4]	4	4	(3)	(3)	[4]	5	4	[4]	[5]	(4)	4	4	3	4	(4)	71	
Sudden-death							4													
Rocco Mediate																				
Round 1 (started on hole 10)	4	4	(2)	(3)	4	4	[5]	3	5	4	3	4	(4)	[5]	4	3	4	(4)	69	
Round 2	4	(3)	3	(3)	4	4	4	3	5	[5]	3	[5]	5	4	4	3	[5]	(4)	71	
Round 3	4	(3)	[4]	4	(3)	4	4	3	5	(3)	3	4	[6]	4	[6]	[4]	(3)	5	72	
Round 4	4	(3)	3	4	[5]	[5]	4	3	5	(3)	3	4	5	(3)	[5]	3	4	5	71	283
Playoff	[5]	4	(2)	4	[5]	4	4	3	[6]	[5]	3	4	(4)	(3)	(3)	3	4	5	71	
Sudden-death							[5]													

◯ Circled numbers represent birdies or eagles.   ☐ Squared numbers represent bogeys or worse.

Hole	Yards	Par	Eagles	Birdies	Pars	Bogeys	Double Bogeys	Higher	Average
1	448	4	0	32	265	149	23	2	4.358
2	389	4	1	65	306	89	10	0	4.089
3	195	3	0	48	309	84	25	5	3.216
4	488	4	0	41	272	143	14	1	4.284
5	453	4	0	69	281	101	18	2	4.159
6	515	4	0	16	245	171	33	6	4.507
7	461	4	1	48	264	136	20	2	4.282
8	177	3	0	30	323	103	12	3	3.227
9	612	5	2	112	285	64	8	0	4.923
OUT	3738	35	4	461	2550	1040	163	21	37.049
10	414	4	0	76	287	93	11	3	4.104
11	221	3	0	35	276	138	20	1	3.310
12	504	4	0	15	209	210	29	7	4.585
13	614	5	7	135	257	64	5	2	4.855
14	435	4	1	58	258	131	18	4	4.253
15	478	4	0	34	270	135	25	5	4.353
16	225	3	0	30	309	119	8	2	3.237
17	441	4	0	46	303	107	10	2	4.185
18	573	5	8	165	234	44	13	4	4.790
IN	3905	36	16	594	2403	1041	139	30	37.676
TOTAL	7643	71	20	1055	4953	2081	302	51	74.725

108th
U.S. OPEN
Past Results

Date	Winner	Score	Runner-Up	Venue
1895	Horace Rawlins	173 - 36 holes	Willie Dunn	Newport GC, Newport, R.I.
1896	James Foulis	152 - 36 holes	Horace Rawlins	Shinnecock Hills GC, Southampton, N.Y.
1897	Joe Lloyd	162 - 36 holes	Willie Anderson	Chicago GC, Wheaton, Ill.
1898	Fred Herd	328 - 72 holes	Alex Smith	Myopia Hunt Club, South Hamilton, Mass.
1899	Willie Smith	315	George Low	Baltimore CC, Baltimore, Md.
			Val Fitzjohn	
			W.H. Way	
1900	Harry Vardon	313	J.H. Taylor	Chicago GC, Wheaton, Ill.
1901	*Willie Anderson (85)	331	Alex Smith (86)	Myopia Hunt Club, South Hamilton, Mass.
1902	Laurence Auchterlonie	307	Stewart Gardner	Garden City GC, Garden City, N.Y.
			Walter J. Travis	
1903	*Willie Anderson (82)	307	David Brown (84)	Baltusrol GC, Springfield, N.J.
1904	Willie Anderson	303	Gil Nicholls	Glen View Club, Golf, Ill.
1905	Willie Anderson	314	Alex Smith	Myopia Hunt Club, S. Hamilton, Mass.
1906	Alex Smith	295	Willie Smith	Onwentsia Club, Lake Forest, Ill.
1907	Alex Ross	302	Gil Nicholls	Philadelphia Cricket Club, Flourtown, Pa.
1908	*Fred McLeod (77)	322	Willie Smith (83)	Myopia Hunt Club, South Hamilton, Mass.
1909	George Sargent	290	Tom McNamara	Englewood GC, Englewood, N.J.
1910	*Alex Smith (71)	298	John J. McDermott (75)	Philadelphia Cricket Club, Flourtown, Pa.
			Macdonald Smith (77)	
1911	*John J. McDermott (80)	307	Michael J. Brady (82)	Chicago GC, Wheaton, Ill.
			George O. Simpson (85)	
1912	John J. McDermott	294	Tom McNamara	CC of Buffalo, Buffalo, N.Y.
1913	*Francis Ouimet (72)	304	Harry Vardon (77)	The Country Club, Brookline, Mass.
			Edward Ray (78)	
1914	Walter Hagen	290	Charles Evans Jr.	Midlothian CC, Blue Island, Ill.
1915	Jerome D. Travers	297	Tom McNamara	Baltusrol GC, Springfield, N.J.
1916	Charles Evans Jr.	286	Jock Hutchison	Minikahda Club, Minneapolis, Minn.
1917-18	No Championships Played — World War I			
1919	*Walter Hagen (77)	301	Michael J. Brady (78)	Brae Burn CC, West Newton, Mass.
1920	Edward Ray	295	Harry Vardon	Inverness Club, Toledo, Ohio
			Jack Burke Sr.	
			Leo Diegel	
			Jock Hutchison	
1921	James M. Barnes	289	Walter Hagen	Columbia CC, Chevy Chase, Md.
			Fred McLeod	
1922	Gene Sarazen	288	John L. Black	Skokie CC, Glencoe, Ill.
			Robert T. Jones Jr.	
1923	*Robert T. Jones Jr. (76)	296	Bobby Cruickshank (78)	Inwood CC, Inwood, N.Y.
1924	Cyril Walker	297	Robert T. Jones Jr.	Oakland Hills CC, Bloomfield Hills, Mich.
1925	*William Macfarlane (147)	291	Robert T. Jones Jr. (148)	Worcester CC, Worcester, Mass.
1926	Robert T. Jones Jr.	293	Joe Turnesa	Scioto CC, Columbus, Ohio
1927	*Tommy Armour (76)	301	Harry Cooper (79)	Oakmont CC, Oakmont, Pa.
1928	*Johnny Farrell (143)	294	Robert T. Jones Jr. (144)	Olympia Fields CC, Matteson, Ill.
1929	*Robert T. Jones Jr. (141)	294	Al Espinosa (164)	Winged Foot GC, Mamaroneck, N.Y.

Date	Winner	Score	Runner-Up	Venue
1930	Robert T. Jones Jr.	287	Macdonald Smith	Interlachen CC, Edina, Minn.
1931	*Billy Burke (149-148)	292	George Von Elm (149-149)	Inverness Club, Toledo, Ohio
1932	Gene Sarazen	286	Phil Perkins	Fresh Meadow CC, Flushing, N.Y.
			Bobby Cruickshank	
1933	Johnny Goodman	287	Ralph Guldahl	North Shore CC, Glenview, Ill.
1934	Olin Dutra	293	Gene Sarazen	Merion Cricket Club, Ardmore, Pa.
1935	Sam Parks Jr.	299	Jimmy Thomson	Oakmont CC, Oakmont, Pa.
1936	Tony Manero	282	Harry Cooper	Baltusrol GC, Springfield, N.J.
1937	Ralph Guldahl	281	Sam Snead	Oakland Hills CC, Bloomfield Hills, Mich.
1938	Ralph Guldahl	284	Dick Metz	Cherry Hills CC, Englewood, Colo.
1939	*Byron Nelson (68-70)	284	Craig Wood (68-73)	Philadelphia CC, West
			Denny Shute (76)	Conshohocken, Pa.
1940	*Lawson Little (70)	287	Gene Sarazen (73)	Canterbury GC, Cleveland, Ohio
1941	Craig Wood	284	Denny Shute	Colonial CC, Fort Worth, Texas
1942-45 No Championships Played — World War II				
1946	*Lloyd Mangrum (72-72)	284	Vic Ghezzi (72-73)	Canterbury GC, Cleveland, Ohio
			Byron Nelson (72-73)	
1947	*Lew Worsham (69)	282	Sam Snead (70)	St. Louis CC, Clayton, Mo.
1948	Ben Hogan	276	Jimmy Demaret	Riviera CC, Los Angeles, Calif.
1949	Cary Middlecoff	286	Sam Snead	Medinah CC, Medinah, Ill.
			Clayton Heafner	
1950	*Ben Hogan (69)	287	Lloyd Mangrum (73)	Merion GC, Ardmore, Pa.
			George Fazio (75)	
1951	Ben Hogan	287	Clayton Heafner	Oakland Hills CC, Bloomfield Hills, Mich.
1952	Julius Boros	281	Ed Oliver	Northwood Club, Dallas, Texas
1953	Ben Hogan	283	Sam Snead	Oakmont CC, Oakmont, Pa.
1954	Ed Furgol	284	Gene Littler	Baltusrol GC, Springfield, N.J.
1955	*Jack Fleck (69)	287	Ben Hogan (72)	The Olympic Club, San Francisco, Calif.
1956	Cary Middlecoff	281	Ben Hogan	Oak Hill CC, Rochester, N.Y.
			Julius Boros	
1957	*Dick Mayer (72)	282	Cary Middlecoff (79)	Inverness Club, Toledo, Ohio
1958	Tommy Bolt	283	Gary Player	Southern Hills CC, Tulsa, Okla.
1959	Billy Casper	282	Bob Rosburg	Winged Foot GC, Mamaroneck, N.Y.
1960	Arnold Palmer	280	Jack Nicklaus	Cherry Hills CC, Englewood, Colo.
1961	Gene Littler	281	Bob Goalby	Oakland Hills CC, Bloomfield Hills, Mich.
			Doug Sanders	
1962	*Jack Nicklaus (71)	283	Arnold Palmer (74)	Oakmont CC, Oakmont, Pa.
1963	*Julius Boros (70)	293	Jacky Cupit (73)	The Country Club, Brookline, Mass.
			Arnold Palmer (76)	
1964	Ken Venturi	278	Tommy Jacobs	Congressional CC, Bethesda, Md.
1965	*Gary Player (71)	282	Kel Nagle (74)	Bellerive CC, St. Louis, Mo.
1966	*Billy Casper (69)	278	Arnold Palmer (73)	The Olympic Club, San Francisco, Calif.
1967	Jack Nicklaus	275	Arnold Palmer	Baltusrol GC, Springfield, N.J.
1968	Lee Trevino	275	Jack Nicklaus	Oak Hill CC, Rochester, N.Y.
1969	Orville Moody	281	Deane Beman	Champions GC, Houston, Texas
			Al Geiberger	
			Bob Rosburg	
1970	Tony Jacklin	281	Dave Hill	Hazeltine National GC, Chaska, Minn.
1971	*Lee Trevino (68)	280	Jack Nicklaus (71)	Merion GC, Ardmore, Pa.
1972	Jack Nicklaus	290	Bruce Crampton	Pebble Beach GL, Pebble Beach, Calif.
1973	Johnny Miller	279	John Schlee	Oakmont CC, Oakmont, Pa.
1974	Hale Irwin	287	Forrest Fezler	Winged Foot GC, Mamaroneck, N.Y.
1975	*Lou Graham (71)	287	John Mahaffey (73)	Medinah CC, Medinah, Ill.

Date	Winner	Score	Runner-Up	Venue
1976	Jerry Pate	277	Tom Weiskopf Al Geiberger	Atlanta Athletic Club, Duluth, Ga.
1977	Hubert Green	278	Lou Graham	Southern Hills CC, Tulsa, Okla.
1978	Andy North	285	Dave Stockton J.C. Snead	Cherry Hills CC, Englewood, Colo.
1979	Hale Irwin	284	Gary Player Jerry Pate	Inverness Club, Toledo, Ohio
1980	Jack Nicklaus	272	Isao Aoki	Baltusrol GC, Springfield, N.J.
1981	David Graham	273	George Burns Bill Rogers	Merion GC, Ardmore, Pa.
1982	Tom Watson	282	Jack Nicklaus	Pebble Beach GL, Pebble Beach, Calif.
1983	Larry Nelson	280	Tom Watson	Oakmont CC, Oakmont, Pa.
1984	*Fuzzy Zoeller (67)	276	Greg Norman (75)	Winged Foot GC, Mamaroneck, N.Y.
1985	Andy North	279	Dave Barr Tze-Chung Chen Denis Watson	Oakland Hills CC, Bloomfield Hills, Mich.
1986	Raymond Floyd	279	Lanny Wadkins Chip Beck	Shinnecock Hills GC, Southampton, N.Y.
1987	Scott Simpson	277	Tom Watson	The Olympic Club, San Francisco, Calif.
1988	*Curtis Strange (71)	278	Nick Faldo (75)	The Country Club, Brookline, Mass.
1989	Curtis Strange	278	Chip Beck Mark McCumber Ian Woosnam	Oak Hill CC, Rochester, N.Y.
1990	*Hale Irwin (74+3)	280	Mike Donald (74+4)	Medinah CC, Medinah, Ill.
1991	*Payne Stewart (75)	282	Scott Simpson (77)	Hazeltine National GC, Chaska, Minn.
1992	Tom Kite	285	Jeff Sluman	Pebble Beach GL, Pebble Beach, Calif.
1993	Lee Janzen	272	Payne Stewart	Baltusrol GC, Springfield, N.J.
1994	*Ernie Els (74+4+4)	279	Loren Roberts (74+4+5) Colin Montgomerie (78)	Oakmont CC, Oakmont, Pa.
1995	Corey Pavin	280	Greg Norman	Shinnecock Hills GC, Southampton, N.Y.
1996	Steve Jones	278	Tom Lehman Davis Love III	Oakland Hills CC, Bloomfield Hills, Mich.
1997	Ernie Els	276	Colin Montgomerie	Congressional CC, Bethesda, Md.
1998	Lee Janzen	280	Payne Stewart	The Olympic Club, San Francisco, Calif.
1999	Payne Stewart	279	Phil Mickelson	Pinehurst Resort & CC, Pinehurst No. 2, Pinehurst, N.C.
2000	Tiger Woods	272	Miguel Angel Jimenez Ernie Els	Pebble Beach GL, Pebble Beach, Calif.
2001	*Retief Goosen (70)	276	Mark Brooks (72)	Southern Hills CC, Tulsa, Okla.
2002	Tiger Woods	277	Phil Mickelson	Bethpage State Park, Black Course, Farmingdale, N.Y.
2003	Jim Furyk	272	Stephen Leaney	Olympia Fields CC, Olympia Fields, Ill.
2004	Retief Goosen	276	Phil Mickelson	Shinnecock Hills GC, Southampton, N.Y.
2005	Michael Campbell	280	Tiger Woods	Pinehurst Resort & CC, Pinehurst No. 2, Pinehurst, N.C.
2006	Geoff Ogilvy	285	Jim Furyk Phil Mickelson Colin Montgomerie	Winged Foot GC, Mamaroneck, N.Y.
2007	Angel Cabrera	285	Jim Furyk Tiger Woods	Oakmont CC, Oakmont, Pa.
2008	*Tiger Woods (71+4)	283	Rocco Mediate (71+5)	Torrey Pines South GC, San Diego, Calif.

*Winner in playoff; figures in parentheses indicate scores

Oldest champion (*years/months/days*)
45/0/15 — Hale Irwin (1990)

Youngest champion
19/10/14 — John J. McDermott (1911)

Most victories
4 — Willie Anderson (1901, '03, '04, '05)
4 — Robert T. Jones Jr. (1923, '26, '29, '30)
4 — Ben Hogan (1948, '50, '51, '53)
4 — Jack Nicklaus (1962, '67, '72, '80)
3 — Hale Irwin (1974, '79, '90), Tiger Woods (2000, '02, '08)
2 — by 15 players: Alex Smith (1906, '10), John J. McDermott (1911, '12), Walter Hagen (1914, '19), Gene Sarazen (1922, '32), Ralph Guldahl (1937, '38), Cary Middlecoff (1949, '56), Julius Boros (1952, '63), Billy Casper (1959, '66), Lee Trevino (1968, '71), Andy North (1978, '85), Curtis Strange (1988, '89), Ernie Els (1994, '97), Lee Janzen (1993, '98), Payne Stewart (1991, '99) and Retief Goosen (2001, '04)

Consecutive victories
3 — Willie Anderson (1903, '04, '05)
2 — John J. McDermott (1911, '12)
2 — Robert T. Jones Jr. (1929, '30)
2 — Ralph Guldahl (1937, '38)
2 — Ben Hogan (1950, '51)
2 — Curtis Strange (1988, '89)

Most times runner-up
4 — Sam Snead
4 — Robert T. Jones Jr.
4 — Arnold Palmer
4 — Jack Nicklaus
4 — Phil Mickelson

Longest course
7,643 yards — Torrey Pines South Golf Course, San Diego, Calif. (2008)

Shortest course
Since World War II
6,528 yards — Merion GC (East Course), Ardmore, Pa. (1971, '81)

Most often host club of Open
8 — Oakmont (Pa.) CC (1927, '35, '53, '62, '73, '83, '94, 2007)
7 — Baltusrol GC, Springfield, N.J. (1903, '15, '36, '54, '67, '80, '93)

Largest entry
9,048 (2005)

Smallest entry
11 (1895)

Lowest score, 72 holes
272 — Jack Nicklaus (63-71-70-68), at Baltusrol GC (Lower Course), Springfield, N.J. (1980)

272 — Lee Janzen (67-67-69-69), at Baltusrol GC (Lower Course), Springfield, N.J. (1993)
272 — Tiger Woods (65-69-71-67), at Pebble Beach (Calif.) GL (2000)
272 — Jim Furyk (67-66-67-72), at Olympia Fields (Ill.) CC (North Course) (2003)

Lowest score, first 54 holes
200 — Jim Furyk (67-66-67), at Olympia Fields (Ill.) CC (North Course) (2003)

Lowest score, last 54 holes
203 — Loren Roberts (69-64-70), at Oakmont (Pa.) CC (1994)

Lowest score, first 36 holes
133 — Vijay Singh (70-63), at Olympia Fields (Ill.) CC (North Course) (2003)
133 — Jim Furyk (67-66), at Olympia Fields (Ill.) CC (North Course) (2003)

Lowest score, last 36 holes
132 — Larry Nelson (65-67), at Oakmont (Pa.) CC (1983)

Lowest score, 9 holes
29 — Neal Lancaster (second nine, final round) at Shinnecock Hills GC, Southampton, N.Y. (1995)
29 — Neal Lancaster (second nine, second round) at Oakland Hills CC, Bloomfield Hills, Mich. (1996)
29 — Vijay Singh (second nine, second round), at Olympia Fields (Ill.) CC (North Course) (2003)

Lowest score, 18 holes
63 — Johnny Miller, final round at Oakmont (Pa.) CC (1973)
63 — Jack Nicklaus, first round at Baltusrol GC (Lower Course), Springfield, N.J. (1980)
63 — Tom Weiskopf, first round at Baltusrol GC (Lower Course), Springfield, N.J. (1980)
63 — Vijay Singh, second round at Olympia Fields (Ill.) CC (North Course) (2003)

Largest winning margin
15 — Tiger Woods (272), at Pebble Beach (Calif.) GL (2000)

Highest winning score
Since World War II
293 — Julius Boros, at The Country Club, Brookline, Mass. (1963) (won in playoff)

Best first round by champion
63 — Jack Nicklaus, at Baltusrol GC (Lower Course), Springfield, N.J. (1980)

Best final round by champion
63 — Johnny Miller, at Oakmont (Pa.) CC (1973)

Worst first round by champion
Since World War II
76 — Ben Hogan, at Oakland Hills CC (South Course), Bloomfield Hills, Mich. (1951)
76 — Jack Fleck, at The Olympic Club (Lake Course), San Francisco, Calif. (1955)

Worst final round by champion
Since World War II
75 — Cary Middlecoff, at Medinah (Ill.) CC (No. 3 Course) (1949)
75 — Hale Irwin, at Inverness Club, Toledo, Ohio (1979)

Lowest score to lead field, 18 holes
63 — Jack Nicklaus and Tom Weiskopf, at Baltusrol GC (Lower Course), Springfield, N.J. (1980)

Lowest score to lead field, 36 holes
133 — Vijay Singh (70-63) and Jim Furyk (67-66), at Olympia Fields (Ill.) CC (North Course) (2003)

Lowest score to lead field, 54 holes
200 — Jim Furyk (67-66-67), at Olympia Fields (Ill.) CC (North Course) (2003)

Highest score to lead field, 18 holes
Since World War II
71 — Sam Snead, at Oakland Hills CC (South Course), Bloomfield Hills, Mich. (1951)
71 — Tommy Bolt, Julius Boros and Dick Metz, at Southern Hills CC, Tulsa, Okla. (1958)
71 — Tony Jacklin, at Hazeltine National GC, Chaska, Minn. (1970)
71 — Orville Moody, Jack Nicklaus, Chi Chi Rodriguez, Mason Rudolph, Tom Shaw, and Kermit Zarley, at Pebble Beach (Calif.) GL (1972)

Highest score to lead field, 36 holes
Since World War II
144 — Bobby Locke (73-71), at Oakland Hills CC (South Course), Bloomfield Hills, Mich. (1951)
144 — Tommy Bolt (67-77) and E. Harvie Ward (74-70), at The Olympic Club (Lake Course), San Francisco, Calif. (1955)
144 — Homero Blancas (74-70), Bruce Crampton (74-70), Jack Nicklaus (71-73), Cesar Sanudo (72-72), Lanny Wadkins (76-68) and Kermit Zarley (71-73), at Pebble Beach (Calif.) GL (1972)

Highest score to lead field, 54 holes
Since World War II
218 — Bobby Locke (73-71-74), at Oakland Hills CC (South Course), Bloomfield Hills, Mich. (1951)
218 — Jacky Cupit (70-72-76), at The Country Club, Brookline, Mass. (1963)

Lowest 36-hole cut
143 — at Olympia Fields (Ill.) CC (North Course) (2003)

Highest 36-hole cut
155 — at The Olympic Club (Lakeside Course), San Francisco, Calif. (1955)

Most players to tie for lead, 36 holes
6 — at Pebble Beach (Calif.) GL (1972)

Most players to tie for lead, 54 holes
4 — at Oakmont (Pa.) CC (1973)

Most sub-par rounds, championship
124 — at Medinah (Ill.) CC (No. 3 Course) (1990)

Most sub-par 72-hole totals, championship
28 — at Medinah (Ill.) CC (No. 3 Course) (1990)

Most sub-par scores, first round
39 — at Medinah (Ill.) CC (No. 3 Course) (1990)

Most sub-par scores, second round
47 — at Medinah (Ill.) CC (No. 3 Course) (1990)

Most sub-par scores, third round
24 — at Medinah (Ill.) CC (No. 3 Course) (1990)

Most sub-par scores, fourth round
18 — at Baltusrol GC (Lower Course), Springfield, N.J. (1993)

Most sub-par rounds by one player in one championship
4 — Sam Snead, at St. Louis (Mo.) CC (1947)
4 — Billy Casper, at The Olympic Club (Lakeside Course), San Francisco, Calif. (1966)
4 — Lee Trevino, at Oak Hill CC (East Course), Rochester, N.Y. (1968)
4 — Tony Jacklin, at Hazeltine National GC, Chaska, Minn. (1970)
4 — Lee Janzen, at Baltusrol GC (Lower Course), Springfield, N.J. (1993)
4 — Curtis Strange, at Oakmont (Pa.) CC (1994)

Highest score, one hole
19 — Ray Ainsley, at the 16th (par 4) at Cherry Hills CC, Englewood, Colo. (1938)

Most consecutive birdies
6 — George Burns (holes 2–7), at Pebble Beach (Calif.) GL (1972)
6 — Andy Dillard (holes 1–6), at Pebble Beach (Calif.) GL (1992)

Most consecutive 3s
8 — Hubert Green (holes 9–16), at Baltusrol GC (Lower Course), Springfield, N.J. (1980)
7 — Hubert Green (holes 10–16), at Southern Hills Country Club, Tulsa, Okla. (1977)
7 — Peter Jacobsen (holes 1–7), at The Country Club, Brookline, Mass. (1988)

Most consecutive Opens
44 — Jack Nicklaus (1957-2000)

Most Opens completed 72 holes
35 — Jack Nicklaus

Most consecutive Opens completed 72 holes
22 — Walter Hagen (1913-36; no championships 1917-18)
22 — Gene Sarazen (1920-41)
22 — Gary Player (1958-79)

79

David Shedloski contributes to a number of golf-based websites and publications, is the editor of *Memorial Magazine* and *NICKLAUS Magazine,* and has authored, co-authored or contributed to four books: *Golden Twilight: Jack Nicklaus in his final championship season; Jack Nicklaus: Memories & Mementos with Golf's Golden Bear* (with Jack Nicklaus); *Obsessed with Golf* (with Alex Miceli); *Golf for Dummies, Second Edition* (with Gary McCord).

The photographers and technicians of **Getty Images** who contributed to this publication are **Jeff Gross, Scott Halleran, Harry How, Rebecca Butala How, Ross Kinnaird, Travis Lindquist, Donald Miralle** and **Doug Pensinger.**

Par and Yardage

Hole	Par	Yardage	Hole	Par	Yardage
1	4	448	10	4	414
2	4	389	11	3	204/221
3	3	142/195	12	4	475/504
4	4	448/488	13	5	614
5	4	453	14	4	267/435
6	4	515	15	4	478
7	4	461	16	3	193/225
8	3	177	17	4	441
9	5	612	18	5	573
	35	3645/3738		36	3659/3905
				71	7304/7643